EPOCHS OF INDIA HISTORY

THE MUHAMMADANS

1001-1761 A. D

EPOCHS OF INDIA HISTORY

THE MUHAMMADANS 1001-1761 A. D

J. D. REES

GYAN

Published by

GYAN

Gyan Publishing House
5, Ansari Road
Daryaganj, New Delhi-110002
Phone: 011-47034999, 9811692060
E-mail: books@gyanbooks.com

Distribution Network
gyanbooks.com
India, USA, Canada, UK, Australia

ISBN: 978-93-7014-305-0 (PB)

First Published, 1894

2nd Impression 2025

Printed at: Gyan Press, Delhi.

EPOCHS OF INDIA HISTORY
THE MUHAMMADANS 1001-1761 A. D
Arthur J. D. REES

Epochs of Indian History

EDITED BY

JOHN ADAM, M.A.

PRINCIPAL OF PACHAIYAPPA'S COLLEGE, AND FELLOW OF THE UNIVERSITY, MADRAS; SOMETIME SCHOLAR OF PEMBROKE COLLEGE, CAMBRIDGE

THE MUHAMMADANS.

1001–1761 A.D.

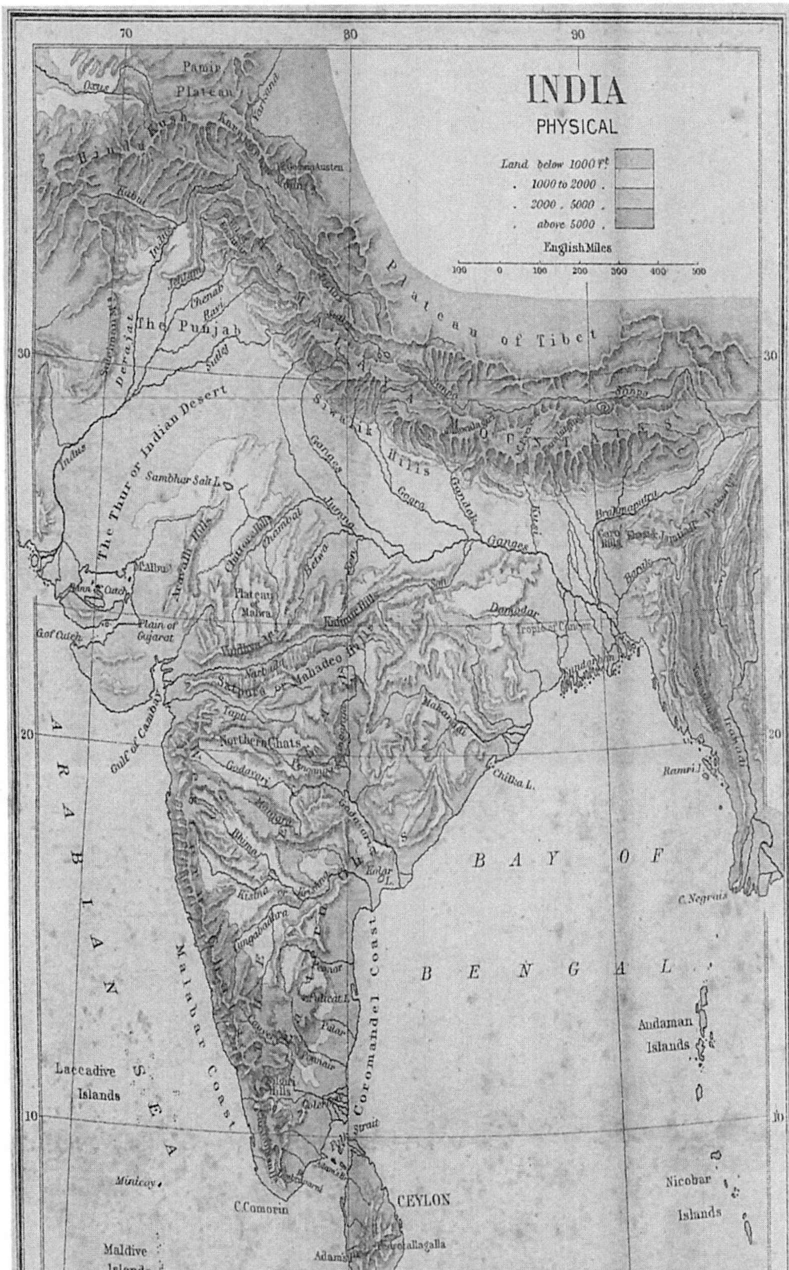

Longmans, Green & Co. London & New York.

Epochs of Indian History

THE MUHAMMADANS

1001–1761 A.D.

BY

J. D. REES, C.I.E., I.C.S.

FELLOW OF THE UNIVERSITY OF MADRAS, PERSIAN AND HINDUSTANI TRANSLATOR TO THE GOVERNMENT, AND SOMETIME TELUGU AND TAMIL TRANSLATOR, MADRAS

AUTHOR OF "TOURS IN INDIA," "H.R.H. THE DUKE OF CLARENCE IN SOUTHERN INDIA," ETC.

WITH THREE MAPS

1894

AUTHOR'S PREFACE.

In writing this little book for the "Epochs of Indian History," I have tried above all things to be brief and comparative. "Whatever else is read, Gibbon must be read," and I have read Gibbon, and have consulted the works of Grant Duff, Sir William Hunter, the Rev. E. Sell, Elphinstone, Ferishta, the Memoirs of Bábar, the Travels of Thevenot, Tavernier, and Bernier, many of the publications of the Hakluyt Society, and such original records as I have been able to consult during seventeen years' residence in the East, during which I have acquired some knowledge of Persian, Arabic, and Hindustani, and have associated with Muhammadans in India, Persia, Turkey, and Arabia. The admirable work of Elphinstone fails, I think, to satisfy the requirements of the ordinary student only because it treats in too great detail the tedious procession of wars and revolts in a great continent, extending over the long period which elapsed between the arrival of the Arabs in India, and the fall of the Mughal Empire. I have endeavoured to mention only such names and events as cannot well be omitted, and as all knowledge is comparative, to focus them by occasional references to contemporary occurrences outside India, for I understand that in this way I can best present a brief narrative of the Muhammadan epoch of Indian history.

J. D. REES.

ST. PETERSBURG, *October* 1893.

TABLE OF CONTENTS

NOTE.

The spelling of proper names is according to the system authorised by the Government of India, except in the case of a few well-known words, as Punjab, Poona, where a change from the customary form would be pedantic. The accent marks a long vowel, and all vowels are sounded as in the Latin languages.

THE

MUHAMMADANS IN INDIA

CHAPTER I.

INTRODUCTION (BEFORE 1001 A.D.)

I. MUHAMMAD AND THE MUHAMMADANS.

MUHAMMAD was born in A.D. 569, and before his death in 632 he had conquered Arabia and made it the home of the faith of Islam, the profession of which is the one and only qualification of a Muhammadan, with whom religion comes before, and above, all national or geographical distinctions, overruling and overriding every other consideration, and ignoring all the divisions that birth, accident, ignorance, or civilization has imposed upon the peoples of the world. In 630 the homeless and friendless fugitive from Mecca, of eight years before, had declared war against the Roman Emperor Heraclius, and the successors of Muhammad had within one hundred years of his death defeated the feeble descendant of Chosroes on the fatal field of Cadesia, founded the city of Bussora, which still owns the allegiance of the Caliph at Constantinople, and sacked the famous city of Ctesiphon, built out of the ruins of Babylon, one solitary arch of which, looking over the Tigris, reminds the traveller of to-day of a far-off Muhammadan period in Turkish Arabia. A fruitless further stand was made by the Persians near Ecbatana of the Medes, in the hill country, on the highway between Babylon and Persepolis, where no traces of former grandeur now remain to attest the greatness of the fall of the successors of Cyrus and Darius. In A.D. 710 the conquest of Khorassan, the western province of Persia, was followed by that of Transoxiana, when, for the first time in history, the Crescent waved upon the banks of the Indus, and the connection of the Muhammadans with India, which has continued through various fortunes till the present day, commenced in the full tide of glory and fanaticism, which spread the faith of Islam from the Guadalquivir to the burning sands of Sindh. Seventy years, however, before this, the Caliph Abubakr had subdued Syria, taking Damascus, Baalbec, and Jerusalem, and Egypt had fallen before the conquering sword of Amron, after the capture of Memphis, when, aided by the Copts, who burned with resentment against the Emperor at Constantinople, he marched to Alexandria, took the commercial capital of the world, and destroyed its priceless library. Meanwhile, the coast of Africa, from the Nile to the Atlantic, was annexed to the Caliphate, and the Moors adopted the language and religion of Muhammad. In A.D. 711 the Muhammadans, under Tarik, the eponymous hero of Gibraltar, crossed the straits, and whether or not aided by a father's thirst for revenge upon the person of the seducer of his daughter, defeated Roderick the Goth at Xeres, and compelled his kingdom of Spain to obedience to the Commander of the Faithful at Damascus, whose absolute, regal, and sacerdotal prerogative, and whose empire, extending from the confines of India and Tartary to the shores of the Atlantic, proclaimed him the greatest monarch of his age. Baffled by Greek fire at Constantinople, the Saracens, or "men of the East," as the Muhammadans were now called in Europe, penetrated into France, and, humanly speaking, would have conquered the whole of Europe but for the arms of Charles Martel, who in A.D. 732 arrested their victorious march in the centre of France, and defeated them in a battle which lasted seven days. The intestine feuds of the Abbasides and Ommiades now occupied the arms and thoughts of the Moslems, and led to the detachment of Spain as a separate monarchy from the Caliphate, and to the dissolution of the dream of universal conquest amidst the pomps and luxuries of Bagdad.

To the era of conquest succeeded one of letters, during which the works of the Greeks were translated into Arabic, and the three rivals who divided the inheritance of the Prophet, the Fatimite in Africa, the Ommiade in Spain, the Abbaside in Bagdad, vied with one another in the encouragement of letters, and so rendered service to the cause of enlightenment, which directly and indirectly kept alight the torch of learning during the long sleep of darkness which had extended from the time of Virgil to that of Almansor, and was to continue in Europe till the days of Dante. During the reign of the Caliph Othman, expeditions had been sent across to the western coast of India in A.D. 636, and later in 662 and 664, but no great results ensued till A.D. 712, when an advance was made into the Indus valley, from which, however, the victorious Arabs were subsequently expelled after witnessing abundant proof of the impotent courage of their Hindu adversaries, who, when worsted in the fight, immolated themselves, their wives, their children, upon colossal funeral pyres. India was now free from the Muslims for upwards of a hundred years, but other nations were to bend or break before their victorious arms. In A.D. 781 the Caliph Harun al Rashid ascended the throne and grasped the staff of Muhammad, but before his elevation he had dictated an ignominious peace to, and exacted a disgraceful tribute from, the helpless Empress Irene, who sat on the Byzantine throne of the Cæsars, the thirty-third successor of Romulus Augustulus, who three hundred years before had resigned the Roman purple to his brother of the Eastern Empire. The same Harun al Rashid, or Aaron the Orthodox, granted the Holy Sepulchre at Jerusalem to Charlemagne, who was crowned by Pope Leo III. in A.D. 800 as Roman Emperor, the Abbaside readily overlooking the fact that Charles had fought against the Saracens of Spain, the kindred of his blood but the enemies of his house, and rejoicing, perhaps, at the elevation of the Frankish king to a position which implied a necessary antagonism to the Byzantine throne, from which he indeed received tribute, but which he had by no means conquered. In A.D. 823 and 827 the Arabs took Crete and Sicily and threatened Rome, while in A.D. 846 their fleets actually ascended the Tiber and spoiled the tombs and temples of St. Peter and St. Paul. The seeds of decay had, however, for some time been evident among the Muslims, and the Caliphs of Bagdad, no longer secure in the love and obedience of their subjects, introduced into the capital a Turkish guard, composed of hardy youths from the uplands of the Oxus, who, either taken in war or bought for a price, adopted the religion of their masters. In A.D. 861 these guards had become dangerous alike to the Caliphs and to their subjects, as the murder of Mutawakel proved, and the approaching ruin of the Saracen Empire was hastened by the excesses of the Carmathians, a sect which, like the Wahabis, and perhaps the Babees, would have reformed reforming Islam with fire and sword, which took Kufa, Bussora, and Mecca, and caused the throne to tremble to its foundations. Meanwhile, Africa, like Spain, was lost to the

Caliphs, and became an independent kingdom under the Aglabites. The Taherites, Soffarides, and Samanides in turn reigned in Khorassan, and Syria and Egypt were usurped by Turkish slaves. In A.D. 933 the throne of Persia was usurped by the Bowides, and in A.D. 936 Moez al Dowlat deposed the last Abbaside Caliph, whose successors reigned merely as pontiffs, with as little real power as was possessed by the titular Mikados, during the supremacy of the military dynasty of the Shoguns in Japan.

In the middle of the tenth century, the Byzantine emperors Nicephorus and Zimisces revenged upon the prostrate Arabs their sieges of Constantinople, and expelled the Saracen princes from many of the most famous cities of Asia, from Antioch, once its capital, and from the venerable Damascus. But the tide rolled back, and though the Abbaside dynasty at Bagdad had fallen for ever, the Muhammadans remained masters of the East; and as early as A.D. 840, by intervening in the domestic discords of Southern Italy, had obtained a footing on the coast of Calabria, and were firmly established in Sicily, from which island they were not expelled till A.D. 1038 by the Normans, who, like themselves, had settled on the confines in Italy of the Western, and of what yet remained to the Eastern Empire, and subsequently recovered Malta, and temporarily broke the Muhammadan power upon the opposite coast of Africa, which, however, exercises our statesmen to this present day.

About the time of the birth of Muhammad, the Turks first burst upon an astonished world from their recesses behind its roof, the high mountains in the centre of Asia, and established themselves as the rulers of Tartary, where they worshipped the genius of air and earth, of fire and water, much as the Shintoists do to-day in

Farther Asia. They took Bokhara and Samarcand on the west, and on the east invaded China, but their loosely consolidated empire lasted only from A.D. 545 to 750, though the emperors of Rome and China paid tribute to its barbarian chiefs, who boasted the lofty title of the Chosroes of Persia, that of lord of the seven climes the earth contains. The broken fragments of this Turkish monarchy existed as separate and independent kingdoms, of the history of which little is known, until Mahmúd of Ghazní (A.D. 1001–1030) asserted the greatness of his race by his seventeen successive invasions of India.

II. The Hindus and Hindustan.

A description of this great country, India, is of course foreign to this work. It will suffice to say that it stretches from the roof of the world beyond the Himálayas to the Southern Ocean, from the eighth to the thirty-sixth degree of latitude, and is nearly 2000 miles in length and in breadth. It is bounded on the north by the Himálayas, on the north-east by Burma, on the north-west by Afghanistan and Beluchistan, and on the east, west, and south by the sea. Within these boundaries are comprised nearly 1½ millions of square miles and 280 millions of inhabitants. Sir William Hunter has admirably divided this extensive empire into three well-defined regions—the Himálaya mountains, the plains of the great rivers that issue therefrom, and the tableland covering the greater part of Southern India. With the first region, which comprises two long parallel mountain walls, rising in places to nearly twice the height of Mont Blanc, this short history of the Muhammadan period has little concern; with the second it is intimately connected; and in the third it has considerable, though less close and continuous, interest.

It is believed that in the times succeeding the Stone Ages, Upper India was peopled by more or less dark-coloured tribes, who were gradually driven southwards by fairer peoples from the north, of the Aryan stock, but whose descendants are still found in the hills of the south and of the Orissa coast, among the wilder races of the Himálayas and the Central Provinces, and even in the hilly country of Lower Bengal. Only two years ago it was suspected that human sacrifices had been offered among the Konds of the wild country of the Eastern Gháts. The tribes found in possession by the invaders from the north are supposed by writers of authority to have entered from the north-east and the north-western passes of the Himálayas, but in fact we still know but little of the earliest inhabitants of India.

The Hindus maintain that the earliest of their Vedas, or historic hymns, was written 3000 years before the birth of Christ, when the eleventh dynasty was reigning in Egypt and the great Pyramid of Cheops had already stood a thousand years; but it is held to be proved by those most competent to form an opinion that its composition cannot be ascribed to an earlier date than 1400 B.C., if indeed there is any satisfactory evidence that the book and the religion of the Vedas existed so long as 800 years before the foundation, in the sixth century B.C., of the religions of Zoroaster, Buddha, and Confucius. To the earliest or Rig Veda succeeded other Vedas and psalms, which exhibit a state of society more nearly approximating to Hinduism as we see it, in which the four castes of Brahman, Kshatriya, Vaisya, and Súdra, or priest, warrior, agriculturist, and serf, appear, in which the Brahman occupies that position of pre-eminence which the advance of education in India under English rule has only tended to confirm. The Brahmans simplified the religion of the Vedas, and made it intelligible to the people as the religion of one God, in three manifestations of Brahma the Creator, Vishnu the Preserver, and Siva the Destroyer, and they absorbed into the Hindu Pantheon the masses of the people who worshipped the forces of Nature and their manifestation in man; and 500 years before Christ, at the time when Æschylus, Sophocles, and Euripides sang in Greece, they had worked out an elaborate system of philosophy, of the science of language, of law, medicine, music, and astronomy, and through the medium of the Arab scholars of the Abbaside court at Bagdad, the fruits of the labours of Brahman sages in the three last subjects were introduced into Arabia and Europe. The Brahmans were also great poets, and the two Indian epics of the Mahábhárata and the Rámáyana are accepted as histories, mixed with fables, of the kings of the Ganges valley, and of the advance of these kings and their followers into Southern India. The former poem relates to events which happened between 1200 and 200 B.C., a period just including the Greek invasions of India by Alexander and his successors. The Pándavas and the Kurus were alike descendants of King Bharata. The five Pándava brothers all had one wife in common, and were all inordinately addicted to gambling, the first, a characteristic of Hindu society, which was faithfully exhibited until quite recent days on the Malabar Coast; the second, a characteristic of the Indians all over India to this day, when the courts in Bombay are engaged in considering whether betting on drops of rain is or is not illegal. So far as chronology will lighten our way, we infer that these princes were engaged in Homeric contests around Delhi two or three hundred years before Homer wrote, just as the princes of India certainly were 2000 years later when the Muhammadans, and 2750 years later when the English, crushed these internecine quarrels by their stronger arms. In the Mahábhárata we find time divided into four ages, during the first of which man lived 100,000 years, during the second 10,000, and during the third 1000 years. In the fourth or Evil Age, the Káli Yúga, in which we live, and in which the poem was compiled, man, for his sins, lives but 100 years. Of this age but 8497 years have elapsed out of 432,000 ; and when the full tale shall have been accomplished, the first age will be begun again, the second, third, and fourth will succeed, and the weary rotation of 4,320,000 years will recommence.

Only to read the interminable and prolix tale is weariness enough. The Rámáyana is more interesting, though few will have the patience to proceed far with either poem in the Sanscrit or in the Indian vernacular translations. Ráma, the eldest son of the king of Oudh, perhaps a thousand years before Christ, bent the great bow as could no other prince, and so proved himself the worthy husband of the Princess Sítá. But palace intrigues, rife then as now in Northern as in Southern India, resulted in the banishment of Ráma and his wife, who wandered southward to the Coromandel Coast, from the jungles of which Sítá was carried off by Rávana, the monster-king of the Golden Isle (Ceylon). Aided by Hanumán, the monkey-general, Ráma recovered his wife, and returned to reign in Oudh. To this day Ráma is the darling hero, Hanumán the favourite general, and Sítá the worthy model of a wife and a princess, to the peoples of India, and their footsteps are marked by temples and memorials from Oudh to Cape Comorin.

Hardly had the Brahmans established their moral and religious ascendency in the land, when Buddha rose, about 540 B.C., to found the religion that still claims more adherents than any other in the world. The sixth century B.C. witnessed also the foundation of the philosophical and moral system of Confucius, and of the religion of Zoroaster, which obtained in Persia, till it was driven out by the Muhammadans, when a small and enterprising minority quitted its fatherland, and settled on the western coast of India, destined to furnish to commerce its most enlightened adherents, to the Legislative Councils of India many, and to the British Parliament, as yet, but one member.

This is no place for a history of the life of Buddha, which in Hunter's luminous prose and Arnold's beautiful verse has become well known, at any rate to all English readers. It will suffice here to say that the prophet was the only son of the king of Kapila, which is placed a hundred miles north of the sacred town of Benáres, who for love of mankind left house and home, and wife and children, to become an outcast and a beggar, till he found salvation, and commenced to offer it to all who would hear the word, which he preached unceasingly till his death in 543 B.C.

His system, which inculcated the efficacy of works and the futility of the mediation of priests and sacrifices, dealt a deadly blow at the priestcraft of the Brahmans, and the two religions were rivals in India till, on the eve of the Muhammadan conquests in the ninth century, the great Hindu heart of India was roused against the reformers, and Buddhism was driven to seek a home in the colder regions north and north-east of the Himálayas, and in the farther east. The faith of the enlightened still holds the field in Nipal, Tibet, Mongolia, Manchuria, Siam, Burma, and Ceylon, while in Japan and China it flourishes side by side with the state code of morals known as Confucianism, the cult of local deities, the forces of Nature, and the worship of ancestors, not the sole, but still the chief religion of the land. In India it absorbed the indigenous tree and serpent worship, and purified and refined the coarser superstitions of aboriginal races. There are still a few Jáins left in India, modern descendants of the Buddhists, and you may see them wearing respirators, lest in breathing they suck down a fly, and deprive an animal of life, and carrying fans wherewith to brush the seat on which they sit, lest unhappily an insect's life be sacrificed. So they conform to the letter of the edicts of King Asoka, who forbade the slaughter of animals, and abolished the indulgence of two peacocks and one deer allowed daily to the royal kitchen. "Meritorious," said this royal reformer, "is obedience towards father and mother, towards friends and acquaintances meritorious is liberality, meritorious is abstention from reviling the heterodox, and meritorious the abstention from killing living creatures."

III. The Greeks and India.

There are yet several subjects that claim attention before the Muhammadans are introduced into the plains of Hindustan. The early tribes and the earliest invaders, non-Aryans and Aryans, I suppose they must be called, and the birth and development of Brahmanism and Buddhism have been briefly noted, but the Greek and Scythian inroads in their turn claim attention.

In the fragments of Ktésías (400 B.C.) which have come down to us, we see the same contempt exhibited of the aboriginal races of India as has been noticed in the great Indian epics. These tribes have the heads of dogs, or are pygmies who were constantly engaged in warfare with cranes, as indeed Homer, five hundred years before, had described them to be. But Ktésías only wrote down what he heard at the court of Persia from travelled Persians or Indians, and till the invasion of Alexander the Great,

327 B.C., we learn little of any value concerning the connection of Greece with India.

In the fragments which have been preserved to us of the *Indika* of Megasthenes, is contained a most interesting picture of the India which was visited by Alexander the Great, the *Indika* having been composed about 300 B.C. Megasthenes says that the inhabitants of the country, having abundant means of subsistence, exceeded the ordinary stature of men, and were distinguished by their proud bearing and skilled in the arts; that all alike were free; that tillers of the soil were unmolested even when battles were raging in their vicinity; and he showed a greater appreciation of the conditions of the continent than is possessed by many writers of the present day when he remarked that India was peopled by races both numerous and diverse. We learn from Megasthenes that all property in India belonged to the Crown, and that cultivators had to pay into the royal treasury a fourth part of the produce of the soil. Touching the manners of the Indians, their frugal method of life excited the admiration of the Greek, and he was struck with the simplicity of their laws and of their contracts; but he could not approve their custom of eating alone, a custom from which, however, and from others connected with eating, even the most advanced reformers of the present day are altogether unwilling to depart. With some natural astonishment, he observes that the Indians accorded no special privileges to the old, unless they possessed superior wisdom. Like Ktésias, he describes the original tribes as dwarfs and pygmies; but foundations of truth can be found for most of his traveller's tales, and there is little in this narrative, written upwards of two thousand years ago, which is more difficult of belief than what the public reads to-day in the histories of African explorations.

Regarding the administration of public affairs, Megasthenes mentions the methodical collection of taxes, the construction of roads, the entertainment of foreigners, and the care of the sick ; and he tells us that births and deaths were registered, trade and commerce encouraged, weights and measures supervised, prices regulated, and that places of public resort received careful attention. The Greek writers identified the gods of the country with their own. They supposed Siva to be Bacchus, and believed Krishna to be Herakles. Megasthenes was probably led into the error of stating that Indian women bore children at the age of seven from the observation of the fact that women of the higher classes are contracted at that age to their husbands, the truth being that they seldom bear children until they are twice that age. But Arrian, who wrote about 150 A.D., says women married at seven and men died at forty. He very faithfully describes the Brahmans and their mode of life, and how they, like Plato, believed the soul to be confined in the body as in a prison together with sensual appetites, with which, during this mortal life, it was bound to struggle in continual warfare. We learn what impression the Indians made upon the Greeks from the well-known answer of the philosopher Dandalis, who said that he had no need of Alexander, whose weapons were powerless against him, since the Brahmans neither loved gold nor feared death.

From the Periplus of the Erythrean Sea, which was probably written about A.D. 90 by a Greek merchant settled in Egypt, we learn something of the commerce of India before the Muhammadan conquest. The historian Pliny, who died in A.D. 79, had described the direct route across the Arabian Sea, which had been discovered by the pilot Hippalos in the reign of the Emperor Claudius. But long before the discovery of Hippalos there had been traffic between the east coast of Africa and the west coast of India, whence rice, butter, sugar, cottons, and muslins were exported. Slaves and horses were imported into India; spices, indigo, and betel-nut were thence exported. Rice, which to this day is called by its Greek name *oryza* (ὄρυζα), *sativa*, and pepper were exported from the northern and southern parts to the western coasts respectively, as were the diamonds of Golkonda, the sapphire, onyx, agate, amethyst, and other precious stones.

Arrian, the historian of the voyage of Nearchus from the Indus to the Persian Gulf, has derived much of his information regarding India from Megasthenes, but in enumerating the castes of the Indians he mentions that of the superintendents, who spy out what goes on in country and town, and report everything to the king. A somewhat similar class of officer exists to this day in the neighbouring empire of China. All these Greek writers on India have much to say about the elephant; and Arrian goes so far to remark that Indian women, if possessed of uncommon discretion, would not stray from virtue for any reward short of the gift of the great beast. The name of Arrian must be mentioned with gratitude, for the voyage of Nearchus opened up communications between Europe and Asia, and the Portuguese did but follow the routes of Alexander's admiral, and the British followed the Portuguese.

These brief references to the Greek writers will show what was the character of the country which Alexander the Great invaded when he crossed the Indus above the great military bridge of Attock and advanced to the Jehlum or Hydaspes, on the banks of which he defeated Porus, one of the monarchs of the Punjab, a victory in memory of which he built Bukephala and Nikaia, the site of the former of which, at any rate, is to this day pointed out to the modern traveller. The conqueror advanced as far as the Beas (Hyphasis), and then returned to the Indus, on which he embarked a portion of his army, while the remainder marched along its banks. At Multan he was opposed by the people of the country, and in the siege of that city he was wounded. At the confluence of the five rivers of the Punjab, on the site of the modern Uchh, he built a town wherein he left a Greek garrison and satrap; and after again embarking upon the river and founding the city of Haidarábád (Sind), he reached the sea, whence he despatched Nearchus up the Gulf to the Tigris, and himself marched through Beluchistan and Persia to the imperial capital at Susa. Part of his army remained in Indian garrisons and a large portion in Bactria, which at his death, two years after his return to Susa, became the inheritance of Seleukos Nikator.

While Seleukos was engaged in founding the monarchy of Syria, Chandra Gupta, an Indian prince, the Sandracottus of the Greeks, was subduing the princes of Northern India, and Seleukos made over to him the Greek conquests in Afghanistan and the Punjab, and stationed at his court the ambassador Megasthenes, to whose writings reference has been made. Antiochus, grandson of Seleukos, entered into a treaty with the Buddhist king Asoka, who has been already mentioned as the grandson of Chandra Gupta. The date of this treaty was 256 B.C., and for a hundred years subsequently the Greek rulers of Bactria fitfully invaded India, but few traces of their domination now remain in the country.

From the date when the Greek invasions of India ceased, those of the Scythians or Tartars, and of the Turks or Turkomans commenced. The tribes of Central Asia then began to make those descents upon the more favoured country to the south, south-east, and south-west of their cold and barren home which culminated in the devastations of Genghis Khan and

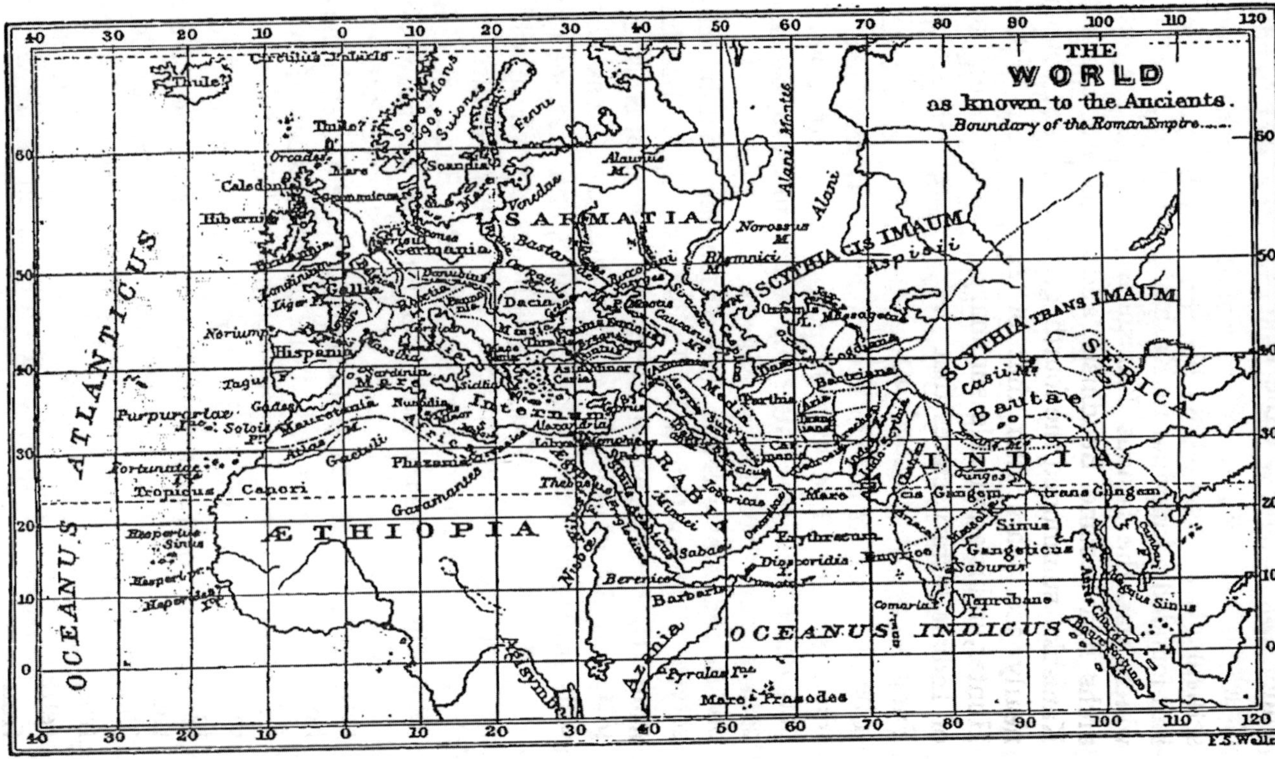
THE
WORLD
as known to the Ancients.
Boundary of the Roman Empire
SARMATIA
SCYTHIA CIS IMAUM
SCYTHIA TRANS IMAUM
SERICA
INDIA
ARABIA
ÆTHIOPIA
OCEANUS ATLANTICUS
OCEANUS INDICUS
Germania
Gallia
Hispania
Dacia
Media
Parthia
Bactriana
Sogdiana
Caspium
Hibernia
Caledonia
Thule?
Scandia
Fenni
Alani
Mare Internum
Mauretania
Numidia
Africa
Canori
Garamantes
Tropicus
Sinus Gangeticus
Taprobane
Mare Erythraeum
Barbaria
Azania
F.S. Weller.

Timur the Tartar. In the beginning they drove out a Greek dynasty from Bactria and destroyed the Greek settlements of the Punjab, and early in the Christian era had founded a kingdom in Kashmir, one of the rulers of which was the famous Kanishka. The Tartar monarchs had become Buddhists, and in 40 A.D. the king Kanishka summoned the fourth great Buddhist council, nearly 300 years after that of Asoka. Sir William Hunter, in his admirable summary of the disputed facts of Indian history, states that the Játs and Dhes of the Punjab are the descendants of the Scythian or Tartar tribes. But, at any rate, it is certain that their inroads were repeated up to the fifth century A.D., prior to which period the indigenous princes strove, with varying success, to withstand them. The Valabhi kings of Gujrat, on the north-west coast of India (500 to 700 A.D.), preserved a precarious independence, and a Chinese pilgrim in 630 A.D. described the court of the Buddhist prince, whose dynasty was overthrown in the eighth century by the first of the Arab invaders of India.

IV. The Scythians or Tartars.

But no history of the Muhammadans in India should thus briefly touch upon the famous annals of the Shepherds of Central Asia, who are generally called by the classical name of Scythians, or by the modern appellation of Tartars. They are divided, according to Gibbon, into four great races. The Mongolian originally came from the country to the north of the great wall of China; the Tungusian, to which the present Manchu dynasty belongs, from the farther north; the Ugrian or Finnish, which settled in the west of Asia, and in the north of Europe, from the Yenesi to Norway, to which branch the Magyars of Hungary belong; and the Turkish, the most famous, which occupies the middle country extending from Lake Baikal to the land of the Slavs. In the third century before the Christian era, the great wall of China was constructed to defend that country from the inroads of the Huns, who belonged to the Turkish branch of the Tartars. In the second century, the Huns, despising the wall, subdued the empire of China; but about 140 B.C. the Chinese threw off their yoke, and in 90 A.D., shortly after the Periplus was written by a Greek merchant who traded with India, the eastern empire of the Huns was broken, the result of successful resistance by the Chinese and of internal dissensions among the Tartar hordes; whereupon they marched towards the Oxus and the Volga, establishing themselves on the eastern side of the Caspian Sea and in the country of the Alani, on the banks of the Volga. After a long period of comparative peace, in which they consolidated their power, the Huns proceeded to make war upon Hermanric, the king of the Goths, after whose death the Ostrogoths submitted to the Scythian Shepherds, and the Visigoths implored the Emperor Valens to permit them to cross the Danube and settle in Thrace, which they did, and whence they in turn waged war upon the Eastern Empire, A.D. 376. In A.D. 410 mercenary hordes of Huns assisted Alaric in the sack of Rome, the advanced guard of the main body of their nation, which had precipitated the Goths and Vandals upon the falling Western Empire. The empire of the Huns now (A.D. 435) extended from the Baltic to the Danube, from the Rhine to the Volga, when Attila, the scourge of God, brought Germany and Tartary under one sceptre, overran Europe from the Euxine to the Adriatic, and ravaged the provinces of Thrace and Macedonia up to the walls of Constantinople, within which the Emperor Theodosius purchased a precarious peace. In 451 A.D. Attila invaded Gaul, and in the following year, Italy. His passage was marked by the pillage of the greatest towns of the north of Italy, the safety of which was purchased by the prospective sacrifice to the embraces of the barbarian of the Princess Honoria, sister of Valentinian, Emperor of the West. The death of Attila in A.D. 453 broke up his empire. His sons divided his territories among themselves. The Goths again raised their heads against the Huns, and they retired into Tartary, and for upwards of a hundred years, till the close of the reign of Justinian, history has little to relate of the so-called Scythian hordes. The Avars were kindred to the Huns, and, like them, were Tartars; and in A.D. 558 they presented to Justinian a petition which he dared not refuse, and flying themselves before the victorious Turks, they offered to support the feeble Byzantines against their barbarian enemies. Ere long the Avars had advanced into Poland and Germany, and encamped upon the Danube and the Elbe. The Turks, however, in turn, offered Justinian an alliance and protection, which he could not refuse, and the Emperor, upon his throne in Constantinople, was bound to dissemble his disinclination to the fateful friendship of either branch of his Tartar allies. In the year A.D. 600, while the successors of Constantine were engaged in defending the frontiers of the Eastern Empire against the arms of the kings of Persia, the Avars reigned supreme from Belgrade to Constantinople. In 614 Chosroes had advanced the Persian limits to the neighbourhood of Constantinople and to the Nile, and on his return from this successful campaign he was invited by an emissary of Muhammad to embrace the religion, which subsequently became that, alike of his country, and of the northern swarms of barbarians, of which the Avars were one branch, while another founded the Mughal Empire in India. During the wars of the Emperor Heraclius with the Persians, the latter entered into a treaty of alliance with the Avars, who in A.D. 626 unsuccessfully besieged Constantinople; whereupon the Roman Emperor made a treaty of friendship with the Turks, with the result that the fate of the empire of the East depended chiefly upon the alliances of the opposing monarchs with different tribes of the Shepherds of Tartary; and no sooner had Heraclius triumphed over the Persians, than the Arab followers of Muhammad commenced to conquer the provinces he had hardly rescued from the successor of Cyrus.

In the history of the Bulgarians can be traced that of the remains of the army of Attila, mixed with the Slavonic tribes of Servia, Bosnia, and Croatia, and their defeat, in A.D. 811, of Nicephorus, Emperor of the East, was avenged a few years later by the arms of Charlemagne, who reduced the Huns of Pannonia.

The Hungarians, as has been said above, belonged to the Ugrian or Finnish branch of the Tartars, which once occupied the greater part of Northern Asia and Europe. They first permanently settled, in A.D. 889, on either side of the Danube, between Belgrade and Vienna, whence they ravaged Bavaria, Swabia, and in 924 invaded Italy to the southern shores of Calabria. Their power was broken in A.D. 934 by Henry the Fowler, Duke of Saxony, and in 955 by the Emperor Otto, after which they settled peaceably in Hungary, and in the ninth, tenth, and eleventh centuries Christianity had spread over that country, together with Bulgaria, Bohemia, Saxony, Norway, Sweden, Denmark, Poland, and Russia. Its progress was marked by the establishment of law and order, and of settled habits of life and government among the Northern barbarians.

CHAPTER II.

THE HOUSE OF GHAZNI (1001–1186).

I. MAHMÚD OF GHAZNI (1001–1030).

IN the previous chapter the rise of the Saracen Empire, its progress and extension towards India, the rise of the Turks and the fall of their empire, the condition of early India prior to, and during the invasion of, the Greeks, and the Scythian or Tartar invasions of India, have been touched upon briefly, and only to such an extent as may be considered necessary to the immediate subject of this little work.

The Tartar Empire referred to in the above chapter had dissolved into its natural condition, and had been disintegrated into separate clans and tribes, dwelling in the country extending from China to the Oxus and the Danube.

In A.D. 650 the Caliph Othman appointed as governor of Kufa, Syed-bin-abu-ul-cas, who, accompanied by the two Imams, Hussein and Hassan, reduced the Persian borders of the Caspian Sea, and converted its inhabitants to the faith of Islam, and soon after the Caliph's governor of Básra subdued the provinces of Seistan, Kohistan, Nishapur, Ghor, Herat, Merv, and Balkh, to govern which conquests he appointed his several generals.

Thus a movement was made towards India, but it was

not till A.D. 664, in the reign of the Caliph Moawiya, that Mohalib Bin Abu Suffra penetrated as far as Multan upon the banks of the Indus, and returned to Khorassan, taking with him many thousands of Hindus destined to become Muhammadans perforce. Eight years later, Abdulla, governor of Kufa, reduced to the faith much of what yet remained of Zoroastrian Persia. In A.D. 683, Khalid bin Abdulla, governor of Seistan, was superseded in his government, and entertaining doubts as to his prospects of returning safely to Arabia through the lately conquered realm of Persia, he retired with a large following into the Suleiman Mountains, where he and his followers intermarried with Afghan converts to Islam. To the chief himself two sons were born, Lodi and Ghor, both destined to found houses famous in the history of India. It was at this time that the Hindus first fought with the Muhammadans in the endeavour to repulse the followers of Khalid bin Abdulla in their attack upon Pesháwar, the plain and hills around which frontier city have till lately witnessed so many hundreds of years of continuous bloodshed. The Hindus repulsed the invaders with such bravery that they were compelled to form an alliance with the Ghakkurs, a tribe of brave mountaineers celebrated in frontier warfare from the days of Mahmúd of Ghazní to those of Ranjít Singh. Thus aided, they were able to advance their outposts to the neighbourhood of Pesháwar, and to build the first of many forts erected to command the famous Kháibar Pass, and thus early the Afghans became a military nation. In A.D. 712 the Arab general Kásim invaded Sindh and settled in the Indus valley, of which the Muhammadans retained possession till A.D. 828; these conquests were, however, but partial and temporary, if indeed more can be said of Muhammadan conquests in any era of Indian history, and it was not till the advent of Mahmúd of Ghazní that anything like permanent occupation occurred.

The Amir or chief, Subuktigín, was a Turk of the household of Alptigín, the governor of Khorassan under the Sámáni dynasty, which ruled over Transoxiana, comprising Khwarism, Joorjan, Khorassan, and Ghazní, the capital of this extensive kingdom being Bokhara. Alptigín made himself independent A.D. 962, and established his capital at Ghazní, and died in 975 A.D., and within two years of his death Subuktigín became his successor, and, following the well-established precedent whereby dependants consolidate themselves in their masters' seats, married the daughter of Alptigín and discovered that he was descended from Yezdijerd, king of Persia. However that may be, his family had for generations been settled in Turkestan, and Subuktigín was, for all practical purposes, as much a Turk as the descendants of Norman nobles are Englishmen. In 977, two years after he assumed the royal style, Subuktigín took Kandahar, and marched over some part of the plain that intervenes between that city and the Indus. He was opposed by Jaipál, Hindu king of Lahore, who marched up to the mountain passes, but suffered defeat. From the tale that a hurricane more destructive to the Hindus than to the hardier Muhammadans was brought on by the defilement of a spring used by the troops of Jaipál, we learn that the Muhammadans had already learned the superstitious reverence of the Hindus for the sacred element of water, which is held to be so pure as to be incapable of acquiring impurity,—an uncompromising opinion, so extreme that in practice it tends to the toleration of impurity. A crushing indemnity in specie and elephants was demanded from, and accepted by, the Hindu Raja, whose Brahman ministers, however, advised him to repudiate the agreement after his return to Lahore.

His generals warned him in vain of the certain resentment and vengeance of Subuktigín, and war broke out afresh, when the Turk descended, as the historian Ferishta says, like a wolf on the fold, and scattered the numerous forces of Jaipál, stationed a garrison in Pesháwar, and after receiving the oath of allegiance from the Afghans, returned in triumph to Ghazní.

The aid of the powerful Subuktigín was now invoked by the youthful Nur, the Sámáni king of Bokhara, who was attacked by one of his rebel officers, and it was stipulated that on the meeting of the royal Nur and the *parvenu* prince, the latter should be excused from dismounting; but when he recognised the features of the royal house in the unfortunate Nur, he threw himself from his horse, and ran to kiss the stirrup of his suzerain.

He did not, however, confine himself to lip loyalty, but defeated the rebel and his allies near Balkh, in an engagement in which his son, the famous Mahmúd of Ghazní, took part.

Subuktigín died at the age of fifty-six, after a successful reign of twenty years, in the year 997 A.D., just when the Emperor Otho III. endeavoured to unite in one wide empire, with Rome as its capital, rude Germany and distracted Italy. He was a brave and just monarch, and the following story will serve to show in what estimation he was held by his contemporaries.

One day when engaged in the chase, he came upon a doe with her fawn, and seizing the latter, he lifted it from the ground without dismounting, as horsemen of the court of the Nizam can do at the present day, and rode off. But the doe followed him with eyes of piteous supplication, whereon he released the fawn, and that night in a dream Muhammad appeared to him and said, "That generosity which thou hast this day shown to a distressed animal has found favour with God, and the kingdom of Ghazní is assigned to thee as a reward in this world. Let not thy power undermine thy virtue, but continue the exercise of benevolence towards mankind."

Another Muhammadan writer states that forty days before his death Subuktigín made the following observations to a friend who sat by his sick-bed :—

"In the exertions we make to avert disease with the hopes of recovery, I am forcibly reminded of the condition of sheep and the butcher. In the first instance the sheep is brought into a strange place, is bound by the feet, and is apprehensive that his end is approaching. After much exertion he submits, and on being shorn of his fleece is allowed to get up and be at liberty; this ceremony is more than once renewed during his life; and lastly, when the moment of death arrives, he permits himself to be quietly bound and resigns his throat to the knife, while he firmly hopes he is only thrown down to be shorn. So we become, in the course of time, accustomed to the bed of sickness; we have recovered so often, that we have no apprehension of danger, till at last death comes suddenly upon us and throws his noose round our necks and we are in an instant throttled."

From the accounts of the invasion of Sindh in 711 A.D. by Muhammad Kásim, nephew of the Arab governor of Basra, we learn of the brave resistance of the Hindus, and particularly of the Raja of Alor, a town which is supposed to have been situated near Bakar, on the east bank of the Indus, where the river is now spanned by the magnificent suspension bridge whereby the railway proceeds to Quetta. The despairing valour of the Rajputs excited the admiration of the Arabs, as it had that of the Greeks. The conquerors called upon the Hindus to pay tribute, and in case of refusal sacked their cities, and put all capable of bearing arms to death; but when tribute was agreed upon, the free exercise of religion was conceded, and even the share of the public revenue which had been allowed to the Brahmans by the Hindu Rajas, was continued by the tolerant conquerors.

The Arabs might have made a permanent settlement in Sindh but for the death and disgrace of the valiant Kásim. In an evil hour he presented to the Caliph Walid, as an offering to the harem, a beautiful daughter of the Indian Raja, who falsely accused him of having dishonoured her, a charge the falsehood of which the Commander of the Faithful learnt too late from her own lips, when the corpse of the brave general was received at Damascus sewn up in a raw hide. Possibly the religious prejudices of, and hatred of change inherent in, the Hindus would in any case have offered a successful though passive resistance to the onward march of Islam, the fanatical spirit of which, already broken by luxury and dominion, was further softened by the mild and tolerant character of Hinduism, which indifferently accords the honorific titles peculiar to its own sacred castes to the English missionary, who, within sight of the most famous shrines of the south, stigmatises the worship held therein as ignorant and senseless idolatry.

In enumerating the early conquests of the Muhammadans, that of Transoxiana, a country in which England and Russia are now so much interested, must not be omitted. A little before the occupation of Sindh, to which reference has just been made, Katiba, governor of Khorassan, led his army across the Oxus, reduced Samarkand and Bokhara, and the kingdom of Khwarism, the modern Khiva. These events were contemporaneous with the conquest of Spain, A.D. 713. One hundred years later Transoxiana had recovered its independence, and the Turkish guards, in whose hands the Caliph was a mere puppet, avenged the conquest of their nation.

The house of Samani, of which Alptigín, the master of Subuktigín, the father of Mahmúd of Ghazní, was a servant, first rose to eminence in the reign of the Caliph Mamun, the son of Harun al Rashid, who long resided in Khorassan, and who appointed members of that family to different governments under his sway. His nominees held their offices long after the authority of the Caliphs ceased to be exercised in Khorassan and Transoxiana, which became their heritage. Alptigín was the slave of Abdul Malik, on whose death he fell into discredit with Mansur, his successor, and retreated to Ghazní accompanied by a body of Mamlukes or Turkish slaves.

Fourteen years later, in A.D. 975, followed his death, the succession of Subuktigín, and his war with the Hindus.

The second son of Subuktigín, Ismail, in the absence of Mahmúd at Nishapur, was recognised as the successor to the throne, but Mahmúd declined to recognise him, and offered the governments of Balkh and Khorassan as a solatium, and on his declining the proposition, defeated him, and assumed the title of king. It is supposed that the dying Subuktigín preferred his younger son, as he was born of a lady of good family, while Mahmúd's mother was a slave. At the present day, for the same reason, the younger son of the Shah of Persia is recognised heir, to the exclusion of the elder and more able prince, the Zil-es-Sultan.

No sooner was Mahmúd installed upon the throne than he sent word to the Samani king of Bokhara of his accession, and asked for confirmation in his father's government of Khorassan; but the king, resenting the independence assumed by the governors of Ghazní, declined, and appointed another governor, whom Mahmúd ejected. Meanwhile internal dissensions at the Samani court resulted in the dethronement of King Mansur and the elevation of Abdul Malik, the creature of the rebel Faik, who was soon deposed by the king of Kashgar, who took all Transoxiana and ended the rule of the Samani dynasty. Mahmúd thereupon married the daughter of Elik Khan and proceeded to consolidate himself in his extensive provinces and in his capital at Ghazní. His fame reached the ears of the Abbaside Caliph at Bagdad, who sent him a robe of honour and the titles of Amen-ul-Millut and Yameen ud Dowlat, or Asylum of the Faith and Right Arm of the State, while Mahmúd in A.D. 1000 assumed for himself the title of Sultan, an old Arabic word for king. Secure in the possession of his kingdom, Mahmúd now looked towards India, the *locus fabulosus* of which Megasthenes had told such wondrous tales; a land of infidels, where the true faith might be extended; an El Dorado, where the dreams of avarice—one at least of the native passions of his mind—might perhaps be realised.

In 1002 A.D., while Ethelred, exasperated by the inroads of the Danes, resorted to the cruel and fatal measure of their massacre in England, Mahmúd of Ghazní was returning from his first invasion of India, in which he defeated Jaipál, the Raja of Lahore, and carried off as a part of the spoil sixteen necklaces, of which one is said to have been worth £80,000. The Hindu Raja, twice defeated by father and son, resigned his crown to his son, Anand Pal, mounted a funeral pyre, and setting fire to it with his own hand, thus terminated his unfortunate existence. Ferishta is the authority for this, and mediæval travellers relate that the Zamorins of Calicut, after a reign of a fixed and certain term, were compelled to ceremoniously cut their throats and make way for their successors.

Two years later Mahmúd returned to chastise the Raja of Bhatiya, who refused to pay his portion of the tribute imposed upon Anand Pal. The Raja, a brave and determined chief, opposed the Muhammadans successfully for three days, but on the fourth, the leaders on both sides devoted themselves to death or victory, and Mahmúd prostrated himself with his face towards Mecca, rose, and shouting "Advance; God is with us," drove the Hindus before him, and the Raja, deserting his fortress, fell upon his own sword in a jungle on the banks of the Indus.

The booty gained in the first and second was, it may be assumed, an additional incentive to a warlike prince to undertake a third expedition, as he did a year later, to reduce to submission the chief of Multan, Abul Fatteh Lodi, who was aided by Anand Pal; but on the defeat of the latter, the Lodi submitted and purchased peace, which was the more readily granted for the reason that the king of Kashgar had invaded Herat, the capital of Khorassan, and Balkh was denuded of its garrison.

Mahmúd behaved in this emergency with the skill and courage of a great general. He left the care of his Indian conquests to a renegade Raja, whose sole hope lay in the protection of the Muhammadans against his own countrymen, marched rapidly to Ghazní, and met Elik Khan near Balkh in a great battle, 1006 A.D., in which the historian relates that the shouts of warriors, the neighing of horses, and the clashing of arms reached the broad arch of heaven, while dust obscured the face of day. Up till that day a Hindu army had always been preceded by a line of elephants, behind which the troops marched; but Mahmúd, knowing that these frightened leviathans wrought confusion to their own side when once turned in flight, so arranged them that, if repulsed, they found unimpeded room for flight behind them. On this occasion, however, they behaved well, and one even seized the standard-bearer of the Tartar king and flung him in the air. Elik Khan was defeated, and Mahmúd, scorning the precept never to make war in the winter, pursued his enemy regardless of the rigour of the weather. A shivering captain entered the tent where the king sat warm and comfortable before a stove, and was greeted with these words, "Go tell the winter he may burst his cheeks with bluster, for here we defy him." The captain went out and delivered the message from the king to winter, and shortly returning said, "I have delivered the message, but the surly season replies, that if his hands cannot reach the skirts of royalty, he will so vex the army that to-morrow Mahmúd shall saddle his horse for himself"; and indeed next day many horses and men had succumbed to the cold, and the victorious Sultan, abandoning the pursuit, returned to Ghazní, and finding that the renegade Raja had revolted, he took him prisoner and confined him for life.

In A.D. 1008 the Sultan resolved to crush his persistent opponent, Anand Pal of Lahore, who implored the assistance of all the Hindu princes, and invoked their aid to expel the Muhammadans from India. So many responded, and so vast an army was collected, that Muhammadans and Hindus confronted each other for forty days near Pesháwar, neither caring to precipitate an engagement. Mahmúd intrenched his camp, and at length began the battle, but his vanguard was turned by the Ghakkar spearmen, who penetrated his camp, but were expelled, when the fortune of the day turned, and the Hindus, losing heart on the flight of their leader, whose elephant fled from the field of battle, were not able to oppose the onslaught of the Muhammadans, and lost, it is recorded, 20,000 on the field. The Sultan next proceeded to take the fort of Nagarkote, situated upon a lower spur of the Himálayas, north-east of Amritsar, in which, on account of its strength, had been deposited "a greater quantity of gold, silver, precious stones, and pearls, than was ever collected in the treasury of any prince upon earth." The spoil has been valued at £313,333—a prodigious amount when the value of money in those days is considered. Mahmúd on his return to Ghazní displayed all his wealth to his people in a great plain outside the city, rewarded his chief captains with titles and presents, and the common folk with feastings and fantasias. But inglorious ease was little to the warrior's taste, and in the following year he conquered Ghor, to the north of Kábul, by the descendants of the king of which country the house of Ghazní was eventually overthrown. The king, Muhammad Ghor, was defeated by means of a simulated flight on the part of his enemies, whereupon he took the poison which he always carried in his signet-ring. The conquest of Ghor formed, however, no obstacle to the continued invasions of India, the sixth of which occupied the year A.D. 1011, and was directed against Thaneswar, a city thirty miles west of Delhi, not far from the Jumna, famous for its sanctity. The Raja of Lahore, Anand Pal, was bound by treaty not to molest Mahmúd and his army, but he sent his brother to represent that, if Thaneswar were spared, he would guarantee the payment of an amount equal to the spoils of its conquest; but the Sultan professed to be, and perhaps was, chiefly animated by a desire to subvert idolatry, and he declined to entertain the proposal, took the city, broke its idols, plundered its temples, and returned with 200,000 captives to Ghazní, the wealth of which was so great that every soldier had many slaves.

The Abbaside Caliph of Bagdad, about this time, at the imperious request of Mahmúd, declared him the lawful sovereign of the whole of the great province of Khorassan, which then extended from Asterabad upon the Caspian Sea to Balkh, and from Yezd, in the centre of Persia, to the desert of Kara Kum. In his seventh invasion of India, Mahmúd followed Jaipál II., now king of Lahore, into Kashmír, and forced the inhabitants of the valley to become Musalmans. The eighth invasion was also directed against Kashmír to punish revolted chiefs, and in returning thence he was misled by his guides, and suffered much loss in men and munitions of war.

But these reverses were succeeded by a glorious campaign in Transoxiana. The nobles of the court of the king of Khwarism had revolted and slain the king. The son-in-law of Mahmúd, who defeated the rebels, annexed the country, took Orgungè, and established himself at the cities of Samarcand and Bokhara, then the most celebrated in Central Asia.

These great events, which extended the Sultan's dominions to the Caspian, took place in A.D. 1016, and in the year immediately following, while Canute reigned in England, one of the greatest of the Indian invasions, the ninth, was carried to a successful conclusion. The great city of Kanouj was situated upon the Ganges, a little to the north of Cawnpur, in the heart of Hindustan, a march of three months from Ghazní, across all the great rivers of the Punjab. The greatness of this city may be inferred from the fact that it is said to have contained 30,000 shops for the sale of betel-nut, as who would say there are 30,000 tobacconists' shops in London! The Raja submitted without a blow to Mahmúd's army of 100,000 horse and 20,000 foot, the latter raised with diplomatic skill among the recent conquests in Transoxiana and elsewhere, soldiers who had been a danger left behind—adventurers whose gain of booty might attach them by the tie of interest to the fortunes of Mahmúd.

The wealth and sanctity of Muttra (Mathurá), a city on the Jumna, north of Agra, next marked it out for attack. Its idols were broken, and the temple was spared only because of its exceeding solidity. The Sultan wrote to his governor of Ghazní, "Here are a thousand edifices as firm as the faith of the faithful, mostly of marble, besides innumerable temples. Such other could not be constructed under two centuries." The Raja of Mahaban, seeing his people massacred and driven into the river, made away with his family and with himself, while the Rajputs of the garrison of another city he attacked, burned themselves and their wives and children. The plunder of this expedition is estimated at £416,000, besides 5300 captives, and 350 elephants, excluding the ruby eyes of idols and their necklaces of pearls and sapphires.

Fired with the ambition of the builder by the sight of so many noble edifices, Mahmúd on his return erected a mosque of marble at Ghazní, so beautiful, covered with such costly carpets, furnished with such gem-encrusted lamps, that it was known as the celestial bride. He also, to his credit in an age and land of ignorance, founded and endowed a library and a museum. The nobility imitated the efforts of their chief, and Ghazní soon became famous for its fountains and its reservoirs, its cisterns and its aqueducts, its mosques, its porches, and its pillared halls. At this time had elapsed nearly 1500 years since the days of the romancers Ktesias and Megasthenes, yet the historian Ferishta mentions as existing then the dove from India which discovered the presence of poison, and the Indian stone which healed wounds. Our descendants will be equally astonished that any credence was accorded to portions of the narratives of Messrs. Du Chaillu and Stanley.

Mahmúd has been chiefly known for his iconoclastic invasions of Hindustan, but the supreme position he occupied among the kings of his day is evidenced by his protection of pilgrims to Mecca. The Sultan employed one of his generals on this escort duty, just as the Government of India employs Messrs. John Cook & Sons at the present day. True, the travellers' friends merely organise expeditions of peace, but they have also been employed in warlike operations, and the progress of caravans to Mecca ever hoped for peace, though prepared for war.

Mahmúd's tenth visit to India (A.D. 1022) was undertaken for the aid of his ally, the Rája of Kanouj, and on his march he defeated Jaipál II., Raja of Lahore, annexed his country, and permanently occupied it by a governor and a garrison, thus laying the foundation of the Muhammadan Empire in India. The eleventh invasion (A.D. 1023) produced little results, and in the following year the Sultan marched to Balkh to dispossess a rebel chief, and started upon the twelfth and most celebrated of all his expeditions, that directed against the great Hindu temple of Somnáth. This shrine was of transcendent sanctity, and the Hindus pretended that the ebb and flow of the Arabian Sea without its walls was but the homage of the ocean. Its massive walls frown over the waters, and can be seen to-day by the passenger from Bombay to Karáchi.

In October A.D. 1024 Mahmúd reached the sultry city of Multan, surrounded by barren sandy wastes, broken here and there by thickets of tamarisk, and there the army prepared for its march across the desert of Sindh to Ajmír—a difficult undertaking—and thence through a more cultivated country to Somnáth, situated upon a narrow peninsula, washed by the sea on three sides. The battlements were manned by the devotees and servants of the god, for such temples are, in fact, no less than towns, of which the holy of holies is the heart, and the temple precincts the centre. The battle raged for three days, and the Muhammadans were yet far from taking the temple-fortress, when Mahmúd prostrated himself before God in the eyes of the army, and praying fervently for victory, led a charge of such violence that resistance became impossible, and the brave garrison abandoned Somnáth to the enemy, leaving 5000 dead behind them. Mahmúd entered the great pillared hall leading to the precincts of the idol, which he approached and broke with his own battle-axe; he sent two fragments of the god to Ghazní, which were seen there 600 years later, when Ferishta wrote his history, A.D. 1612. The Brahmans implored the conqueror to spare the idol, and offered him a prodigious bribe for his clemency, but he replied that he desired that his name should go down to posterity as "Mahmúd the destroyer, and not as Mahmúd the seller, of idols"; and his wisdom as well as his zeal were proved when the broken stone disclosed within its recesses a vast treasure of precious gems. The staff of this great temple included 2000 Brahman priests, 500 dancing-girls, 300 musicians, and 300 barbers. The last-named functionaries were required to shave devotees before their entrance into the sanctum. The Hindus leave unshaven the one spot that the Catholic priest shaves; the Buddhist shaves the whole head. Among the Christians the tonsure probably perpetuates the crown of thorns; among the Hindus it probably originated in some cleanly observance. The Babylonians practised the tonsure, and the priests of Osiris shaved their heads. The tonsure, as a symbol of hierarchy, can be traced back to the times of the Accadians, and there is no cause for wonder in the existence at Somnáth of so large a staff of barbers.

After defeating the Raja of Nehrwala, Mahmúd rested

his victorious arms at the capital, the chief town of Gujarat, which was so much to his taste that he entertained an idea of making it the seat of his government, and a base whence he might extend his sway over Ceylon and Pegu. The ancient names of these countries, Sarandip, or the Golden Isle, and the Golden Chersonese, sufficiently supply the motive for the projected conquests. Wiser counsels, however, prevailed, and Mahmúd selected to govern Gujarat in his absence a prince who had adopted the life of a hermit. There was, however, another prince of the same family, from whom the Sultan's nominee apprehended trouble, and the latter besought Mahmúd to take his enemy away to Ghazní, to which city a return was now imperative after an absence of two and a half years. Mahmúd decided to march from Gujarat to Multan across the desert, and, misled by his Hindu guides, suffered intolerable tortures from thirst and heat. The unfaithful pathfinders, put to the torture, confessed that, to avenge the injuries of Somnáth, they had brought these troubles on the destroyer of that sacred shrine. At last, however, the Muhammadan army reached Ghazní, A.D. 1026, and one of the first petitions presented to Mahmúd proceeded from the prince-governor of Gujarat, who prayed that his foe might be delivered into his hands, now that he sat secure on his viceregal throne. Reluctantly, for the captive prince had won his regard, Mahmúd complied, and the inhuman viceroy dug a vault under his throne in which to confine his rival, his principles not permitting him to shed blood. The presence of the captive graced or disgraced his progress to his capital, till he lay down to rest under a tree. The chroniclers relate that he spread a red handkerchief over his face and lay alone sleeping, when a vulture, thinking the kerchief a piece of gory meat, swooped down upon it and destroyed the eyesight of the sleeper beneath, who thereon, as a blind man, incapacitated from reigning, was consigned to the vault he had dug for his rival, who mounted the throne.

Mahmúd's thirteenth and last invasion of India, was undertaken to chastise the Jats of the Punjab, who had opposed his return from Somnáth. He is said to have routed his enemies in a naval engagement on the Indus, at the same spot where Alexander equipped his fleet for his long homeward sail, thirteen hundred years before.

But the victorious arms of the Sultan were now to encounter a worthy foe in the Seljuk Turks, who for the first time crossed the Oxus and invaded his dominions. Mahmúd in 1027 defeated the horde, which was soon, however, to subdue all Persia and Asia Minor, and conquered Irak, and left his son Musáúd governor of Ré, at the ruins of which, near Teheran, a solitary tower alone remains to testify to the grandeur of a once magnificent capital. So little does the Persian Government appreciate its interest, that not long since it had been furnished with a varnished door and a brass knocker.

The conquest of Persian Irak, which, besides Ré, includes the famous cities of Kashan, Ispahan, "Half of the World," and Hamadan, Ecbatana of the Medes, raised the power of Mahmúd to its highest pitch of glory. The Buyades, or Bouides, or Dilemites, had risen to eminence in the woods of the Caspian province of Mazenderan between 932 and 1055, seized Western Persia from the Samani predecessors of Mahmúd, and Bagdad from the Caliph, in whose name they professed to rule. At this time their sceptre was in the hands of a widowed princess, who wrote to Mahmúd to say that her defenceless condition afforded her a protection which she might have sought in vain in the arms of her powerful husband. She was, whether from motives of policy or clemency, permitted to reign as long as she lived, when her dominions were annexed by Mahmúd. But the great conqueror had now in turn to meet his master, and on April 29, 1030, in his city of Ghazní, to quote the words of Ferishta, he yielded up his body to death and his soul to immortality, amid the tears of a sorrowing people. Two days before his death, all his wealth of gold and precious stones were paraded before his closing eyes, his chariots and led horses, his camels, his elephants, and all the pomp and paraphernalia of the greatest king of the epoch. He gave away nothing, and shed tears at the prospect of leaving his hoards. Hence the tale of the poet Sadi, that a certain one saw Mahmúd, hundreds of years after his death, in a dream. His body was indeed bereft of flesh, but the eye of covetousness still burned brightly in its sunken socket, as if still seeking to amass further treasures.

Many tales are told of the inflexible justice of this great king. One will suffice, and it is one known to all students of that Persian literature which owes so great a debt of gratitude to Mahmúd. A poor man complained that one of his courtiers came to his house in pursuit of his handmaiden, and the Sultan told him to complain the next time this outrage was committed. The man obeyed, and Mahmúd took his sword, slew the intruder in the darkness, and calling for a light, thanked God, and called for food and drink. The suppliant said: "My lord, why didst thou first extinguish the lamp, and why didst thou thank God on seeing the face of the man who wronged me, after thou hadst slain him, and why didst thou need food at this unreasonable midnight hour?" The Sultan replied, "I put out the light, lest, seeing the face of my son, the hand of justice might be stayed, for I thought no other had dared to be so bold; and when I found it was not he, I thanked God; and indeed I had need of food and drink, for I had sworn to abstain from both till such time as I had seen thee righted."

Of his conscientious appreciation of the duties of a sovereign the following story supplies an example. The mother of a merchant, slain by robbers in an outlying province, complained to Mahmúd, who pleaded the difficulty of preserving order in so remote a part of so large an empire, but confessed himself in fault when the petitioner boldly replied, "Why then do you conquer countries which you cannot rule, and deny that protection to its people for which you are responsible before God?"

Mahmúd was fortunate in possessing an able minister in Abúl Abbás Fazíl, who introduced the practice of using Persian as the official language, to which measure is attributable the frequent use of Persian expressions in administrative affairs, which survives from Kábul to Cape Comorin in the present day. The court of Ghazní was the retreat of scholars as well as the school of generals. There flourished four hundred poets, including Ferdousi, author of the "Sháh-Námah," and the philosopher Unsuri, who first acquired the favour of the monarch by composing some acceptable lines on the tresses of his favourite mistress. The "Sháh-Námah" owes its inception to the Sultan, who desired that the heroic legends and deeds of Persia should be worthily commemorated in an epic poem. Dakíki undertook the work, but shortly died, whereupon Ferdousi succeeded him, on a promise of a golden coin for every verse. When the immense work was concluded, a silver coin only was paid, which so incensed the poet, that he fled from Ghazní, and wrote a satire on the avarice of Mahmúd and the immorality of his mother. Perhaps an intimation that a poem, however good, might be too long, was intended. However that may be, the "Sháh-Namah" remains the great epic poem of Persia, and is a well of Persian pure and undefiled, if indeed the profuse use of Arabic words and quotations, which characterises later authors, can be termed defilement. No Muhammadan considers an introduction of the sacred tongue of the Koran as other than advantage and ornament combined.

Mahmúd has been handed down to posterity as remarkable for avarice and bigotry, but in fact the latter vice is hardly proved against him, when the fervid spirit of Islam, four hundred years after the death of its founder, is taken into account, and he probably slew as many Muhammadans in Persia as Hindus in India. This however proves the less, as the hatred between different sections of one has ever been greater than that between two religions.

Of the state of society at the court of Mahmúd, and of the condition of the countries under his government, little information exists, but in the kingdom of Ghazní proper and in the realm of Persia the population were chiefly Persians, the *personnel* of the administration and the troops of the army being chiefly Turks, with still a large infusion of the Arab element. Mahmúd himself was a Turk on his father's and a Persian on his mother's side. After the conquest of Transoxiana large numbers of Turks had been employed in the business of government and in offices of trust both military and civil, and the guards of the kings of the day were chiefly composed of Turkish slaves or Mamluks. Society was thus composed of widely varying elements, which acted and reacted one upon another. The Turks were brave, hardy, and obedient; the Arabs proud, violent, and fanatical; the former cared little for religion or literature, to which the latter were passionately attached. The Persians were then, as they are now, artful and ingenious, polished and untrustworthy. They adopted the religion of Muhammad with haste and with warmth, and their beautiful yet simple language has been, and still is, the chief channel of polite intercourse and literature in Muhammadan Asia. The authority of the Sultan was probably well established in the towns, and elsewhere varied according to the character of the country-folk and the ability of their rulers, just as it does to this day in the dominions of the Shah; and in the hilly country the hardy tribesmen were probably as independent then as they are now in the Bakhtiyari country, in Kurdistan, and in Afghanistan, and were in Beluchistan till the English lately reduced them to submission to a firm yet conciliatory yoke. In India the authority of Mahmúd was probably as ill defined as that of China in Thibet, let us say, at the present day. The army of Mahmúd is said to have included 54,000 horse and a contingent of Hindu cavalry. In his time the Turks as a nation had not adopted the faith of Muhammad, but the Mamluks were invariably forced or willing converts to Islam.

II. Muhammad to Kuru Malik (1030–1186).

Sultan Mahmúd left two sons, twins. The elder by a few hours, Musáúd, though possessed of those qualities of daring and reckless bravery which might have been expected to endear him to his father's heart, was passed over by him in favour of the younger and more docile brother, Muhammad, who ascended the throne A.D. 1030. His elder brother, when informed of this event, wrote saying he had no desire to acquire by force the kingdom their father, notwithstanding the claims of seniority, had been pleased to confer on the younger brother, he himself being amply dowered with the provinces his own sword had won, but that he must insist that in the Khutba, or public prayer for the king, read daily in every mosque, his name should be first mentioned. Muhammad not only refused to comply with this demand, but, contrary to the advice of his counsellors, who doubtless were aware of the strong public feeling in favour of Musáúd, defied his brother, who then advanced from Ispahán. His army deserted to Musáúd, who caused Muhammad to be seized, blinded, and imprisoned, and himself ascended the throne five months after his father's death, A.D. 1030.

And now the Seljúks, who had long threatened the empire, rose to power, and the new king found his post no sinecure. The origin of this tribe is not very well known, but, from the records that have descended to us, it would appear they derived their name and origin from one of the great Tartar chiefs, who, having incurred the enmity of his sovereign, had emigrated with his followers to Jáund on the left bank of the Jaxartes, whence they moved southwards into Khorassan, the first Turkish horde that had as a united tribe or nation permanently fixed its location south of the Oxus. The reign of Masáúd, which lasted from 1030 till 1040, was chiefly spent in war with the Seljúks, whose general, Tóghral Beg, defeated him near Merv, whence he retreated across the Indus, only to be deposed and succeeded by his blind brother, Muhammad. This defeat was of great import to the history of India, for it made dominions which had previously been a mere appanage of Ghazní the chief territory of that great house. The Seljúks occupied Herat, Kistan, and Ghor, and Tóghral moved westward to conquer Persia and Mesopotamia, and to threaten the Byzantine Empire. Módúd, the son of Masáúd, succeeded Muhammad, and by a prudent marriage deprecated and diverted the hostility of the Turks. The Sultan needed friends, for the

Raja of Delhi rose against him and laid siege to Lahore, the chief garrison of the Muhammadans in India, which, however, successfully resisted the attack.

The reigns of the ten last kings of the house of Ghazní were not remarkable for any events of great importance in the progress of the Muhammadan power in India.

After the death of Módúd dissensions arose among the principal chiefs with regard to the succession. The infant son of the late king Masáúd, a child of four years, was raised to the musnud by Ali Bin Rubua, as a first step towards his own usurpation of the throne, which was prevented, however, by Aluptigín Hajib, one of the chief warriors of the court of Módúd, who attacked and defeated Ali, and caused Abul Hasan Ali, a son of the Sultan Musáúd, and brother of the late king, Módúd, to be placed on the throne.

Abul Hasan Ali ascended the throne A.D. 1049, and married the widow of his brother Módúd. Ali Bin Rubua, having plundered the treasury, fled the country, and, after raising a large army at Pesháwar, took Multan and Sindh, and subdued the Afghans, who had latterly plundered these provinces. Ali Rubua held them independently of the crown till A.D. 1051, when Abul Rashid, son of the Sultan Mahmúd, advanced on Ghazní, and having deposed his nephew, whose power had been gradually declining, himself ascended the throne. Abul Hasan's reign extended over two years only.

Almost the first act of the new king was to induce Ali Bin Rubua to return to his allegiance, while Nostugín Hajib, who had been of great service to him in gaining the throne, was despatched with an army to Lahore, where he took the town of Nagarkote, which had fallen into the hands of the Hindus.

Tógral Hajib, another chief, who, having married a daughter of the Sultan Módúd, was by him raised to the rank of noble, was also sent to Seistan, then in open rebellion. He promptly quelled the revolt, but the man who departed from Ghazní an apparently loyal chief, at the bidding of the king, returned to it ere many weeks were over in the guise of a declared rebel and aspirant to the throne. It is related that being asked what first induced him to aspire to the crown, Tógral replied that as Abul Rashíd ordered him to proceed to Seistan, he observed that his hand trembled, and then he concluded that the hand that shook at the revolt of a province was unfitted to grasp and retain a kingdom.

Such was Tógral, who managed to raise an enormous army and marched on Ghazní, which he took, and caused the king, and, as he thought, all the princes of the house of Ghazní, to be put to death. He forcibly married a daughter of the Sultan Musáúd, and his ambitious hopes were all but realised, when a conspiracy headed by Nostugín and other nobles put an end alike to his dreams of glory and his life. He was assassinated on the steps of the throne on the New Year's day of the Persian year, after a brief reign, if it may be so called, of forty days.

Nostugín now by public proclamation called any prince of the house of Ghazní, if so be one survived, to come forward and claim the crown, when it was discovered that no less than three princes had escaped the cruelty of Tógral owing to their imprisonment in a fort at the time of the royal massacre. They drew lots for the throne, and the prize fell to Farokhzád, who accordingly was proclaimed king, A.D. 1052.

Farokhzád at once handed over the administration of affairs to his trusty general Nostugín, who soon had to defend Ghazní from the attack of the Seljúk chief, Jakur Beg Daoúd, who advanced at the head of a large army, but was defeated with great slaughter by the Ghaznivides. Emboldened by this victory, Farokhzád next advanced on Khorassan, which also succumbed to his victorious arms, many prisoners being taken, including the chief leader, Kulbarik. But now Alp Arslán, son of Jakur Beg Daoúd, placed himself at the head of the Seljúks, determined to retrieve these repeated defeats, and after a sharp encounter succeeded in routing the Ghaznivides and taking several of their leaders prisoners. However, on Farokhzád's releasing Kulbarik and the other Seljúk captives, Jakur Beg allowed the Ghazní prisoners also to depart.

In A.D. 1057 Farokhzád narrowly escaped assassination by his slaves in the bath, and by his personal gallantry alone frustrated their design. In the following year, however, he died, after a reign of six years.

Farokhzád was succeeded by his brother Ibrahím, A.D. 1058, another of the three surviving princes, who was "remarkable for devotion and morality, having in his youth subdued his sensual appetites"—notwithstanding which he left a family of thirty-six sons and forty daughters, the latter of whom, we are told, he bestowed in marriage on learned and religious men.

He was a prince of intellectual rather than martial tastes, and the libraries of Mecca and Medina still possess two copies of the Koran written by himself and presented by him to the Caliph. Almost his first act was to make a truce with the Seljúks, to whom he ceded all the countries they had conquered, on condition that they forbore to press their conquests any further, at least in the direction of Ghazní. The treaty was also cemented by the marriage of his son Musáúd with the daughter of the Seljúk chief, Mulik Shah Suljuki.

In A.D. 1079 Ibrahím marched into India, and in the course of his reign added several new towns and forts to the already large number which acknowledged the Muhammadan power, including the forts of Ajudhan and

Rudpal, and the town of Dera near Multan. Dera defied the invaders for over three months, but eventually the town was taken by assault after a siege accompanied by much slaughter on both sides.

The town was found to contain great riches, and the victorious Muhammadans returned to Ghazní laden with booty, besides the 100,000 prisoners they are reported to have taken.

It is recounted of Ibrahím that one day while inspecting the progress of a new palace he had ordered to be erected, he came upon one of the 100,000 prisoners staggering pitifully along beneath the weight of a huge stone. Struck with compassion, he bade the poor wretch drop his load, and there and then gave him his liberty. Now it happened that the stone was dropped in the midst of a much-frequented highway, where it became a fruitful source of accidents to, and imprecations from, passing travellers; but none dared remove it, as it had been dropped there by order of the Sultan. At length a noble who had experienced a fall from his horse by reason of the obnoxious obstacle ventured to suggest to the king that its removal would confer a benefit on the public; but the king replied, "I commanded it to be thrown down and left there; and there it must remain as a monument of the calamities of war, and to commemorate my sense of its evils. It is better for a king to be pertinacious in the support even of an inadvertent command than that he should depart from his royal word." And years later, in the reign of the Sultan Behrám, the stone was pointed out, and the story told of the decision of the eccentric king.

The date of Ibrahím's death is uncertain, but it is supposed to have occurred either A.D. 1089 or 1098. Ibrahím was succeeded by his son Musáúd, a prince of many excellent qualities, who revised all the laws of the state, remodelling the code on improved principles. During his reign the Muhammadan conquests were extended beyond the Ganges farther than they had been carried by any king since the time of Mahmúd. At this time Lahore may be said to have become the capital of the empire, the repeated incursions of the Seljúks having gradually rendered untenable the more ancient strongholds of the house of Ghazní in Iran and Turan.

The reign of Musáúd II. was undisturbed by either foreign or domestic broils. He held his court during part of his reign at Lahore, and after a reign of sixteen years he died A.D. 1114. Some records state that he was succeeded by his son Kumal ud Dowla Shiruijad, who had barely ascended the throne when he was assassinated by his brother Arslán, while other histories pass straight on to Arslán without mention of Kumal ud Dowla. But Arslán was soon deposed by Behrám, who enlisted the aid of the Seljúks, and reigned till 1152, a patron of letters and the friend and protector of the poet Nizámi. It was this prince who caused the fables of Pilpay or the Anwar-i-Soheili to be translated into Persian, thereby causing their eventual dissemination over most parts of the world. A Hindu king had originally sent a copy of the work in the original Sanscrit to Nowsherawan the Just, king of Persia, whose minister is said to have invented the game of chess to teach his master that in the game of government foresight was of more import than chance, and that the pawns of life require attention as well as the more considerable pieces. The book, in turn, was used by the minister as a proof that wisdom and cunning are always more than a match for mere brute force. The Sultan Behrám twice visited India for the purpose of reducing rebellious governors and collectors of the revenue—that is to say, officers responsible for the revenues as well as for the administration of the districts intrusted to their charge by supreme authority, in which sense the word "collector" continues to be used in the British administration of India. But an impolitic act of cruelty brought disgrace on Behrám and ruin on his house. The kingdom of Ghor was tributary to that of Ghazní, and its prince had married the daughter of Behrám, who, notwithstanding this alliance, seized him and put him to death; thereon his brother Seif-ud-Tui drove Behrám from Ghazní, but subsequently falling into the hands of the deposed king, together with the Ghorian minister, a descendant of the Prophet, suffered a shameful death at his hands. The king of Ghor, with blackened face, seated upon a bullock, and looking towards the animal's tail, was paraded along the streets of Ghazní, and finally beheaded, while the minister was impaled. But the brother of the unhappy prince, Alá-ud-dín of Ghor, at once made war on Behrám, saying it was no new thing for kings to make war upon their neighbours, but that such barbarity as this was unknown. The Sultan might know that God had forsaken him, and that Alá-ud-dín, the humble instrument of the Almighty, would soon depose him from the position he had disgraced. He was as good as his word, and the defeated Behrám died in obscurity, while his splendid capital, adorned with the spoils of Hindustan and enriched by the lavish expenditure of successive sultans, was delivered over to fire and sword. The house of Ghazní was still represented by Kushrú, son of Behrám, who retreated to Lahore, and there reigned until 1160; and with his son, who continued to exercise a feeble authority over the miserable remains of the empire of Mahmúd, the house of Subuktigín came to an end in 1186, when the king of Ghor marched into India and took Lahore.

Alá-ud-dín disgraced his triumph by his cruelty.

Ghazní burned for seven days, and the blood of its saints was used for mixing mortar for the erection of monuments of victory in Ghor, while its destroyer gained for himself the title, universally adopted by historians, of Jahánsóz—"Burner of the World."

CHAPTER III.

AFGHANS AND TURKS (1186-1526).

I. HOUSE OF GHOR (1186–1206).

I CAN afford but little space for a brief outline of the house of Ghor. So contradictory are the various accounts on this subject, that were I to describe it in detail, my narrow limits would be speedily outstepped.

There seems to be no doubt that the family was of Afghan origin, though one historian asserts that the Ghoris were Turks and came from Khita; while others trace their descent from Suri and Sam, two brothers of the house of Zohak, one of the fabulous kings of Persia.

Wonderful are the tales of the adventures of Sam and his son Hussain Suri. Ferishta relates in all good faith how Sam, the head of the house of Sur, not long after the time of Mahmúd, was shipwrecked and drowned; how his son shared a plank with a tiger for three days—not such an improbable story as it may appear to those who have not had opportunities of witnessing the behaviour of wild animals during the convulsions of nature. How his son, Eiz-ud-dín Hussain, was condemned to death by Sultan Ibrahím of Ghazní, but was pardoned and married to a princess of that house, and placed by Sultan Musáúd in charge of the dependent principality of Ghor. One of his sons was Alá-ud-dín, who destroyed Ghazní, as related in the last chapter, and was himself defeated by Sultan Sanjar, head of the Seljúks, who in turn was defeated by the Euzes of the Turkish tribe of Kipchak. The Seljúk governor of Khwarizm revolted against the Seljúk king, and called in the aid of the Khitans, a tribe from Northern China. The invasion of the Khitans pushed the Turks of Kipchak farther west, and precipitated their advance into Syria and the Byzantine Empire.

Seif-ud-dín, the son of the Incendiary of the World, Alá-ud-dín Jehansoz, reigned but one year, and was succeeded in 1157 by Ghíyás-ud-dín, his cousin, who associated with him in the task of government his brother Muhammad Shaháb-ud-dín, who took advantage of the decline of the Seljúk power in that part of its dominions to annex Eastern Khorassan, after which Herat became one of the Ghorian capitals. In 1176 Muhammad marched upon Multan and besieged Uchh, in scaling the walls of which Alexander the Great had been wounded.

Muhammad, anticipating the Austrian maxim, "Let others gain by war, but Austria by marriage," finding he could not take the fort by force, offered marriage to the Raja's wife. She replied that she herself was too old, but that her young and blooming daughter should be the Sultan's bride as soon as she had assassinated her husband and opened the gates, which she presently did. Now, Muhammad knew what trust to place in a woman who was false to her husband, and profiting by her perfidy, he drove her forth from the country she had betrayed. Let no one suppose this princess a fair representative of Indian womankind, which is in general remarkable for chastity and honour, and of which individual heroines will compare favourably with those of any clime and country. After another successful expedition into Sindh, Muhammad advanced upon Lahore, now the capital of Khusru Málik, the last of the house of Ghazní, and took him captive. The prisons of princes were then, even more than at a later date, too near their graves; and with the death of Khusru and his family the house of Ghazní became extinct in 1186.

Muhammad now was left face to face with the Hindus, and did not subdue the Rajput principalities without a severe struggle. Indeed, some were never subdued, and remain, actually or nominally, independent to the present day. The feudal and military system of the Rajputs admirably fitted them to successfully resist an invader. As every chief owned an allegiance, which was the pride of his life, to the sovereign, so every chief's retainers entertained the same feeling towards himself. Like the Arabs, they set a high value upon the virtue of hospitality, and, like all fighting races, they greatly esteemed the bards by whose poems their doughty deeds were to be handed down to posterity, as those of their ancestors had been in the martial pages of the Mahábhárata.

The four greatest Indian princes at the time of the invasion of Muhammad were the kings of Delhi and Ajmír, of Kanouj and of Gujarat. A quarrel between the first two Rajas soon afforded the welcome pretext for Muhammadan intervention, and Muhammad met the king of Delhi, called the Prithur Raja, near Thaneswar, 1191, at a place called Tirowri, when the Sultan and the Raja of Ajmir met in single combat, and the latter's teeth were driven down his throat by the lance of the invader. But personal prowess availed not, and Muhammad, deserted by most of his captains, had to retreat to Lahore, and thence to Ghor, where he made every officer who had played him false march around the city wearing nosebags containing grain, which they were compelled to eat, like horses.

In 1193 he again marched into India with an army of 120,000 Turks and Afghans, after an interval of two years, during which, notwithstanding external appearances, he neither slept at ease, nor awoke but in sorrow and anxiety, and never departed from his determination to retrieve his lost honour. Prithur Raja, with a vast army belonging to the confederate Hindu princes, awaited his approach and urged him to return, saying that if weary of his own life, he might yet be willing to save his troops from the rank-breaking elephants, the plain-trampling horses, and blood-drinking soldiers of the Hindus. The Sultan, affecting a fear he little felt, by a timorous answer inspired his foes with such confidence that they spent, in riot and debauchery, a night the Muhammadans devoted to rest and prayer, and were totally defeated on the morrow. Leaving a slave, Kutab-ud-dín, in possession of his Indian conquests, the Sultan marched to Ghor, but in the following year (1194) again returned to India to defeat the Raja of Kanouj on the banks of the Jumna, and to take his capital city and the sacred Benares, in whose thousand temples he cast down the idols and desecrated the symbols of Hindu worship.

The army of Ghor's invasion of India had now become almost an annual event, and in 1195 Muhammad besieged and took Gwalior, but returned to Ghor in 1196 on the death of his brother Ghíyás-ud-dín, upon the occurrence of which event he assumed the title, as he had long exercised the power, of king of Ghor, and was presently engaged in contests with the king of Khwarizm, who contested with the house of Ghor the supremacy of Central Asia. At first he was victorious, but the Khwarizmians, by the aid of the Khitan Tartars, defeated him in 1203, whereon the turbulent Ghakkars of the Sewalik mountains attacked the Muhammadans.

The historian Ferishta dwells upon the wild and cruel character of these tribes, which in later times have continually proved a frontier difficulty. He says they had neither religion nor morality, that is, it may be supposed, to a Muhammadan's mind. When a female child was born, she was carried to the door of the house by a person who held a knife in his disengaged hand, and it was signified that if any one wanted a wife she was available, and if not, she was food for the knife. The scarcity of women thus resulting was counterbalanced by the prevalence of polyandry, such as exists to this day in parts of India. To Muhammad Ghori is attributed the glory of the defeat and conversion to Islam of these barbarians, by murderers or patriots of whose race he was, however, assassinated in 1206, as he lay in his tent on the banks of the Indus, enjoying the cool close of a sultry day. Thus died Muhammad Ghori, thirty-two years after he succeeded to the government, and three years after he mounted the throne. He was a great conqueror and worthy to be named with Mahmúd of Ghazní, whose house he overthrew, and whom he resembled also in a love of accumulating treasure. In that he failed to patronise men of letters, he failed also to hand down his name and fame to posterity with the glory that surrounds the great king of Ghazní.

Though Mahmúd Ghori was proclaimed the successor of his uncle, the empire of Ghor at once dissolved, and three Turkish slaves of the deceased Sultan became independent in their respective governments, Kutab-ud-dín in India, Eldoz in Ghazní, and Nasir-ud-dín in Sind. Mahmúd retained only Ghor and Eastern Khorassan, which a few years later were taken with Ghazní by the kings of Khwarizm. So ended the house of Ghor, in 1215.

II. Contemporary Western Muhammadans.

From this point the history of India has little connection with that of countries west of the Indus, and this affords a convenient opportunity for glancing at the history of the Muhammadans to the west of Persia and Central Asia, which in these pages has received no attention since the close of the first chapter. It was there related how the Emperor Heraclius had hardly triumphed over the Persians and made an alliance with the Turks, when the Arab followers of Muhammad commenced to conquer the provinces he had hardly rescued from the successor of Cyrus, while the Prophet yet lived; how between 636–651 Persia, between 632–639 Syria, in 639–641 Egypt, in 647–709 Northern Africa, and in 711–713 Spain, in turn were conquered by the arms of the Muhammadans, who in 668 appeared for the first time before the walls of Constantinople, and in 718 subdued the south of France and reached the banks of the Loire, whence they were turned back by Charles Martel; how Spain revolted in 750, and the Caliphate was divided into three branches under the Ommiades, the Fatimites, and the Abbasides. Harun-al-Rashid, Caliph of Bagdad, the greatest prince of his race, humbled the Empress Irene in Constantinople and reigned from 781 to 805, the ally of Charlemagne and the patron of learning. In 823 the Arabs conquered Crete and Sicily, and in 846 menaced Rome. But as the conquerors mingled with the conquered, they lost the courage and fanaticism they brought from their desert home in Arabia, and engaged the hardy Turk to fight their battles and to guard their princes; till weakness and luxury and the swords of the Carmathian sectaries dissolved the falling empire of the Caliphs, which split up

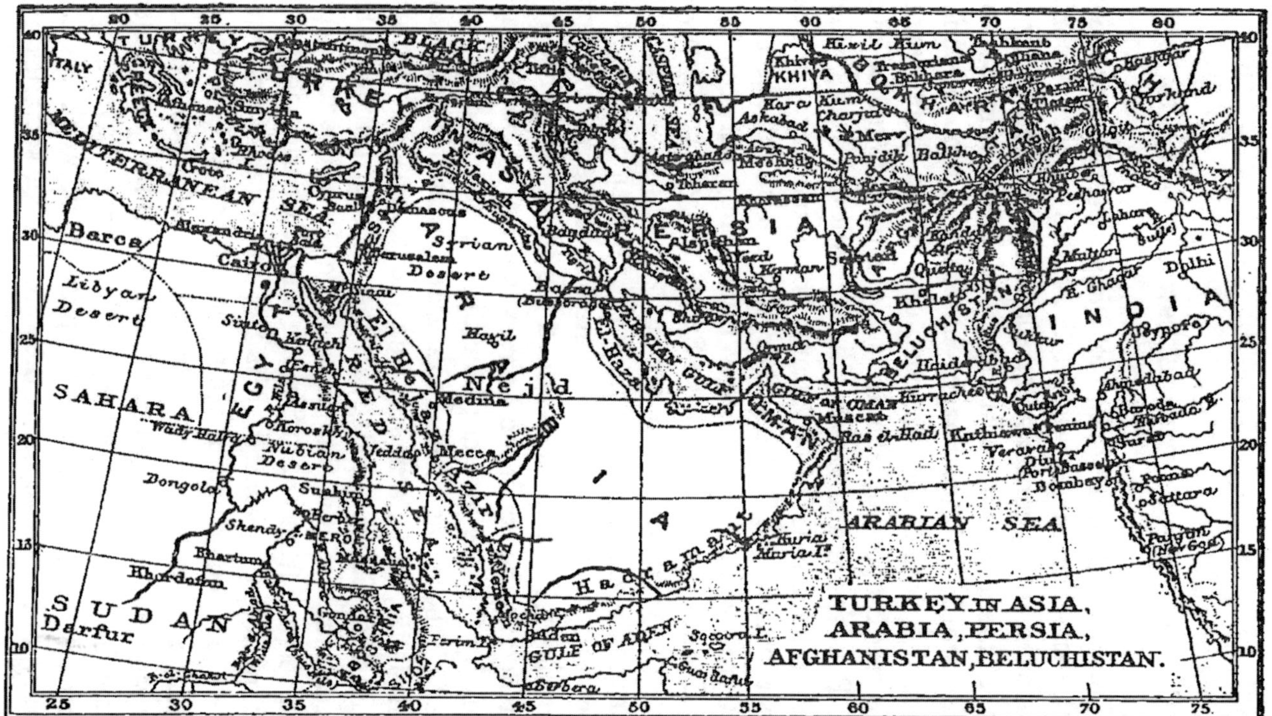
TURKEY IN ASIA,
ARABIA, PERSIA,
AFGHANISTAN, BELUCHISTAN.
BLACK SEA
CASPIAN SEA
MEDITERRANEAN SEA
PERSIA
INDIA
BELUCHISTAN
ARABIAN SEA
GULF OF ADEN
SAHARA
SUDAN
Darfur
Libyan Desert
Syrian Desert
Nubian Desert
Nejd
El-Hasa
OMAN
KHIVA
Kizil Kum
Barca
Cairo
Alexandria
Damascus
Jerusalem
Medina
Mecca
Jedda
Hayil
Dongola
Shendy
Khartum
Suakin
Bagdad
Ispahan
Yezd
Kerman
Askabad
Merv
Meshed
Teheran
Balkh
Herat
Kandahar
Quetta
Khelat
Multan
Delhi
Jeypore
Ahmedabad
Surat
Bombay
Poona
Sattara
Kurrachee
Haiderabad
Muscat
Ras el Had
Kuria Muria Is.
Socotra I.
Aden
Cutch
Kathiawar
Khorassan
Bokhara
Kashgar
Yarkand
Peshawar
Cyprus
Crete
Rhodes
Smyrna
Kordofan
Wady Halfa
Korosko
Assuan
Siwah
Sukkur
Mohammerah
ITALY
TURKEY
GREECE
T. S. Waller

into various fragments in Spain, Africa, Fez, on the west; while the Taherites (813-872) became independent in Khorassan, to be overthrown by the Soffarides, who reigned till 900, when they were overthrown by the Samanis, the fortunes of which house are more fully narrated in Chapter ii.

The Buyade princes took Persia and held it from 933 to 1055, reducing the successors of Muhammad to the position of slaves, whose authority had been usurped in Egypt and Syria by the Fatimite Caliphs. The Greek emperors of Constantinople now rose in arms and crossed the Euphrates, invaded Syria (961), and approached the neighbourhood of the Tigris, and in 1038 the Normans wrested Sicily from the Arabs for the Grecian Emperor. At this time, to quote the words of Gibbon, the name of Turk or Turkman was still famous among the Greeks and Orientals, and though their Scythian empire of the sixth century had long since been dissolved, the fragments of the nation, each a powerful and independent people, were scattered over the desert from China to the Oxus and the Danube; the colony of the Hungarians was admitted into the republic of Europe, and the thrones of Asia were occupied, as has been shown in the last two chapters, by slaves and soldiers of Turkish extraction. They overran Persia, and their princes of the house of Seljúk erected a splendid empire from Samarcand to the confines of Greece and Egypt, and their dominion was maintained in Asia Minor till the victorious Crescent was planted on the dome of St. Sophia.

The career of Mahmúd, one of the greatest of the Turkish princes, has been fully narrated in these pages, and it has been seen how between 997-1028 he enlarged the boundaries of his kingdom from Transoxiana to Ispahan, and from the shores of the Caspian to the mouth of the Indus; and how his son Musáúd was overthrown and defeated by the Turkmans from the eastern side of the Caspian Sea.

These Turkmans elected as their chief Tógral Beg, the grandson of Seljúk, who drove the Ghaznivides westwards towards the Indus, embraced, with his followers, the religion of Muhammad (1038–1063), and was declared by the Caliph at Bagdad the temporal vicegerent of God upon earth. Tógral justified this title by delivering the successor of the Prophet from the tyranny of the Buyade princes of Persia (1055), and by invading the eastern provinces of the Byzantine Empire, with the courage of the Tartar hordes and the fanaticism of recent converts to Islam. In 1063 the nephew of Tógral Beg, Alp Arslán, succeeded him, and during his reign of ten years he wrested from Constantinople the fair provinces of Armenia and Georgia, took prisoner Romanus Diogenes, the consort of the Empress Eudocia, after defeating the armies of the Byzantine Empire, expelled the Arabs from Jerusalem, and in 1072 was about to reduce to submission Turkestan, the home of his race, when he was slain by the dagger of an assassin, saying with his last breath, "I was advised by a sage to humble myself before God, to distrust my own strength, and never to despise the most contemptible foe. I have neglected these lessons, and my neglect has been deservedly punished."

Alp Arslán, who was a contemporary of William the Conqueror, was succeeded by his son Malik Shah, who reduced Transoxiana to obedience to the house of Seljúk and took the great cities of Samarcand and Bokhara. The hordes of Turkestan obeyed the genius of the Shepherd king, whose rule was acknowledged alike in far Kashgar, on the borders of China, in the hills of Georgia and Armenia, in Persia, in Syria, in parts of Arabia, and up to the confines of Constantinople. But upon his death in 1092, his vast empire was divided into the kingdoms of Persia, of Kirwan, of Syria, founded upon the ruin of the Arabian principalities of Aleppo and Damascus, and of Roum, the first permanent settlement of the Turks in the Eastern Empire. In 1074 the Turks laid waste the so-called Roman, or rather Byzantine provinces up to the shores of the Hellespont, and intervened on behalf of one of the rival claimants to the Byzantine throne, and from that day forward the kingdom founded by Soliman was known as that of Roum, or the Muhammadan dominion in Rome, a grievous establishment for the Church and Empire. The limits of the new kingdom extended from the Euphrates to Nice in Bithynia, 100 miles from Constantinople, and from the Euxine to the borders of Syria, for it was not till 1076 that the Seljúks were established in Jerusalem. Since the Caliph Omar had taken the Holy City, the Arabs or Saracens, as they were called in Europe, had not interfered with the devotions of Christian pilgrims, who had also been protected by Charlemagne and his successors, and more recently by the Fatimite Caliphs of Egypt, the Christian republic of Amalfi, the Knights of the Hospital of St. John, and in a fitful and intermittent manner by the emperors of Constantinople. With the one exception of the desecration of the Sepulchre in 1009 by the mad Fatimite Caliph Hakem, of whose followers the Druses alone remain, no violence had ever been done to Christian feeling by the successive rulers of Syria. But when the Seljúk dominion commenced, the command of the Holy City was entrusted to a Turkoman chief named Ortok, who insulted the pilgrims, dishonoured the patriarch, and gave such provocation to the Christians that Europe soon resounded with their appeals for protection and cries for vengeance; and so it happened that it was against the Turks in Syria and in Asia Minor that Peter the Hermit, and Pope Urban II., and Alexius the Emperor, directed the disordered enthusiasm against the infidel, and desire for war and rapine, which took form in Europe in the first Crusade (1096). Since the death of Malik Shah and the division of his inheritance, which has been above narrated, the disorders of the Turkish Empire had prevented a continuous and successful resistance to the Franks, and the Caliph of Egypt, in 1098, seized the opportunity to expel the Turks from Jerusalem, and to restore Palestine to the sceptre of the Fatimites, the Crusaders protesting meanwhile against the usurpation by either branch of the followers of Muhammad of the Holy Sepulchre, of which in the following year they became possessed upon the capture of Jerusalem by Godfrey of Bouillon and his confederates. The Turkish kingdom of Roum was now cut off from Syria, and its capital removed from Nike to Iconium, 300 miles from Constantinople. Upon the fall of the Seljúk Sultans, their slaves, according to Asiatic precedent, rose to eminence from their ashes, and Nur-ud-dín, son of a servant of the Seljúk, in 1145, reigned from the Nile to the Tigris, and it was by his successes in the East that St. Bernard's fears for the Holy Sepulchre were excited to such a pitch of fever as resulted in the second Crusade, in which Louis VII. of France, the Emperor Conrad, and the kings of Poland and Bohemia took part. The great Salah-ud-dín or Saladin, the capture by whom of Jerusalem was the cause of the third Crusade (1189), was the nephew of Sir Acoh, a Kurdish general of Nur-ud-dín, who took Egypt from the imbecile Fatimite Caliph in the name of the Abbaside Caliph at Bagdad, in whose name in turn he professed to reign at Damascus. On the death of Nur-ud-dín, Saladin openly assumed the independent sovereignty of Egypt, and vexed the Christians in Syria, and the Sultan who succeeded Nur-ud-dín at Damascus. The siege and fall of Acre, the march of the Emperor Barbarossa through Asia Minor, and the alliance and rivalry of Philip Augustus of France and Richard I. of England, are foreign to this narrative, and too far remote from the fortunes of the Seljúks, where Eastern and Western history meet in the twelfth century, albeit Frederick Barbarossa besieged and defeated the Sultan in his capital at Iconium, and was himself harassed throughout his homeward march, and until his death in a mountain torrent of Cilicia, by hordes of Turkmans.

The fourth Crusade (1203) was diverted from Syria to Constantinople, the feud between the Greek and Latin Churches, and the Emperor and the Latin princes, having been developed and increased by their meeting and by their interests, now common and now different, as they appeared from time to time in the progress of the Crusades. The taking of the imperial city by the French and Venetians, the elevation of Baldwin, Count of Flanders, to the imperial throne, and the short and troubled reigns of the Latin Emperors of Constantinople (1203–1261), do not properly fall within the compass of this narrative, but the fifth Crusade, 1218, was directed against the Muhammadans of Egypt, in the hope that from the reduction of that country the fall of Palestine would necessarily follow. In 1228 the Emperor Frederick II. made a treaty with the Sultan whereby Christians and Muhammadans were allowed equal rights to the unmolested exercise of their respective religions in Jerusalem, and this arrangement continued in force till 1243, when the Khwarizmians, flying before the Mongols, hurled their relentless arms upon Syria, and overcoming the Frankish and Arab princes alike, pillaged the Holy City and profaned the Holy Sepulchre.

The sixth Crusade of St. Louis (1249) found the Sultan of Egypt protected and oppressed by his Mamluk slaves, the hardy progeny of Tartary and Turkestan, and the seventh (1269), in which he lost his life, resulted only in the glorious but unavailing conquests of Prince Edward of England, who delivered Acre, dictated a truce, and returned home to conquer Wales and Scotland.

The Mamluk Sultans of Egypt soon retook all the conquests of the Crusaders, and in 1291 Acre, their last remaining stronghold, fell, and the Christian churches of Syria were demolished.

III. Slave Kings (1206–1288).

To return to India. From the date of the dissolution of the house of Ghor, that country became an independent kingdom, and ceased to have any connection with countries west of the Indus. Kutab-ud-dín Aibak, the Indian viceroy who became independent at Delhi upon Muhammad Ghori's death, was a Turki slave, bought by a merchant who presented him to his master. He reigned in Delhi twenty-four years, during twenty of which he was the representative of the king of Ghor. He was brave and accomplished; the fact that he was kind and considerate to those about him may be inferred from the legend that his white elephant died of sorrow soon after he did; and that he was a good sportsman is evidenced by the manner of his death, from a fall at polo, in 1210.

An incompetent son of Kutab-ud-dín, whose name still survives in that of the graceful column of the Kutab Minar near Delhi, was soon removed, and Ghamo-ud-dín Altamsh, a Turkish slave of Kutab-ud-dín, succeeded. He is said to have been of noble family, and to have been sold by slave brokers for no less than 50,000 pieces of silver on account of his personal beauty. Eldoz, another Turkish slave, who had succeeded to the Ghazní portion of Muhammad Ghori's dominions, affected to have succeeded to his empire, and presently being driven out of Ghazní by the king of Khwarizm, he made war against Altamsh, but was defeated and made prisoner.

At this time the famous Ghengiz Khan, with the united hordes of Tartary, invaded Khwarizm, laid waste the country, and either slew or enslaved its inhabitants. The Sultan fled to an island in the Caspian ; his son opposed the Mughals to the banks of the Indus, and then sought the help of Altamsh. The Mughals, having approached the confines of India, pursued the prince of Khwarizm into Sindh, and the aggressors were unsuccessfully resisted by Nasir-ud-dín, another Turkish slave of Muhammad Ghori, who had become independent at Multan. Nasir-ud-dín soon after was defeated by Altamsh, and Sindh for the first time, in 1225, was permanently subjected to Muhammadan rule. To the crown of Delhi were soon added Behar and Bengal, the Muhammadan prince who governed these provinces having claimed to be an independent sovereign.

Altamsh next (1226) reduced all Malwa, the country around the Vindhya mountains, to obedience, after which all Hindustan proper was subject to the throne of Delhi, though the native princes or Muhammadan deputies were more or less dependent or independent according as the character of king and of prince or deputy varied. Like Mahmúd of Ghazní, Altamsh was a great iconoclast, and he destroyed the vast temple of Kali in Ujain, and broke its idols before the door of the mosque at Delhi. This able and enterprising prince was succeeded in 1236 by a worthless son, Rukn-ud-dín, who was speedily deposed by the chief nobles of the court, who placed upon the throne the eldest daughter of the late king, Sultan Raziya Begum, of whom the historian Ferishta says, that those who scrutinise her actions most severely will find in her no fault but that she was a woman. Her father had remarked that, though a woman, she had a man's heart and head, and was better than twenty such sons as God had given him. She gave great offence, however, to the proud Muhammadan nobles by making her master of horse, an Abyssinian slave, Amir-ul-Omrah, or chief of the nobles, and by permitting him to lift her upon her horse, than which no greater familiarity was proved to exist between them. The head of the discontented was a Turki chief called Altúnia, but him she married, and for a while made way against her enemies, when her brother Behrám defeated her armies, putting her and her husband to death, and reigned but two years, when he himself met with the same fate.

The reign of Behrám's successor, Ala-ud-dín Masáúd (1241–1244), is remarkable only for the eruption in the latter year of the Mughals into Bengal by way of Thibet.

The grandson of Altamsh, Nasir-ud-dín Mahmúd, now ascended the throne, and his vizier was the well-known Ghíyás-ud-dín Balban, a Turki slave, who had married a daughter of his sovereign's grandsire, a man of great capacity, who in 1247 reduced to submission the Hindu Rajas around Delhi, the bonds of whose obedience had been relaxed during the late reign, and kept back the Mughals, who now held all the lands across the Indus. The Warden of the Marches, Shir Khan, even expelled the Mughals from Ghazní for a season. The greatness of Ghíyás-ud-dín earned the envy of other nobles, and for awhile he was dismissed from power, but presently returning, again repulsed a Mughal attack on the Punjab in 1253, and in 1266 received in great state, on behalf of his nominal master, who died that year, an ambassador of Holáku, grandson of the great Ghengiz Khan.

Nasir-ud-dín lived a life of austerity, and made his sole queen cook his meals. One day she burnt her fingers, and asked for a maid to help her, but the king declined, on the ground that he was but the trustee of the revenues of the state. He advised patience, and promised reward on the day of judgment. This severe monarch elected to eat only what he could buy with the fruits of his penmanship.

Ghíyás-ud-dín Balban now assumed the title, as he had before possessed the power, of king, and he at once proceeded to put to death such other Turki slaves as had risen to eminence, and might prove dangerous to himself. Having slain possible enemies, he proceeded to make friends, and his, the only Muhammadan court not overthrown by the Mughals at the time, soon became the asylum for the princes of Roum, Turkestan, Khorassan, and Persia, who had been expelled from their dominions by the hordes of Ghengiz Khan. Different quarters of the capital long preserved memorials of the asylum of the Muhammadan world, in their names of Abassi, Khwarizmi, Delimi, Atabaki, Ghori, Rumi, Kashghari, Changizi, and others, among which will be found the names of most of the great Eastern houses referred to in the previous pages. Meanwhile, the protector of the victims of the Tartars, was himself protected by a mercenary Tartar guard. The king's creed was that monarchs can be saved only by the exercise of four duties. They must assume dignity and exercise power at proper seasons; punish immorality and indecency; select good men as the officers of justice; and be patient and just themselves in its administration. Ghíyás-ud-dín preserved game and forbade the manufacture of spirituous liquors. He was a patron of letters, and the great poet Sádí, in his old age, sent him a present of his works from the bowers of Musalla.

In spite of his pomp and power, Ghíyás was troubled with insurrections in Mewát, where he is said to have put 100,000 persons to the sword, and in the Doab. Notwithstanding this severity, he did not forget those who had served him, and having granted to certain officers past their work pensions of half their pay, a rate now usually obtaining, he subsequently ordered the disbursement of full pay on the representation of a venerable magistrate, who said, "If in the presence of God old men are rejected, what will become of me?"

In 1279, Tógral Khan, the Viceroy of Bengal, revolted, but the king, after some want of success at first, finally routed him, after a daring and successful campaign, in which forty heroes penetrated into the heart of Tógral's camp, and created such a panic as led to the flight of his army. On his return to Delhi, he learnt that the Mughals had invaded Multan, and the heir-apparent, Prince Muhammad, was despatched to oppose them. The parting advice of the king to his son is so truly an Eikon Basilike, that it may be transcribed in full from the pages of Ferishta, even in so small a work as this. Little knowing that the prince was destined to predecease his father, he took him aside and said:—

"I have spent a long life in the administration and government of kingdoms; and some knowledge I have acquired which may be of service to you after my death, which in the course of nature must now soon happen.

"When you shall ascend the throne, consider yourself as the deputy of God. Have a just sense of the importance of your charge. Permit not any meanness of behaviour in yourself to sully the lustre of your station, nor let avaricious and low-minded men share your esteem, or bear any part in your administration.

"Let your passions be governed by reason, and beware of giving way to anger. Anger is dangerous in all men, but in kings it is the instrument of death.

"Let the public treasure be expended in the service of the state with that prudent economy, yet benevolent liberality, which reason will dictate to a mind like yours, ever intent on doing good.

"Let the worship of God be inculcated by your example, and never permit vice and infidelity to go unpunished.

"Be ever attentive to the business of the state, that you may avoid being imposed upon by designing ministers.

"Make it your duty to see that they execute your commands without the least deviation or neglect, for it is through them you must govern your people.

"Let your judges and magistrates be men of capacity, religion, and virtue, that the light of justice may illuminate your realms.

"Let no levity on your part, either in public or private, detract from that important majesty which exalts the character of king; and let everything around you be so regulated as to inspire that reverence and awe which will render your person sacred, and contribute to enforce respect to your commands.

"Spare no pains to discover men of genius, learning, and courage. Raise not a low man too hastily to a high station, lest he forget himself and be an eyesore to men of superior merit.

"Never attempt anything, unless through necessity, but what you are sure to accomplish; and having once determined upon a measure, let your perseverance be never shaken, nor your mind be ever averted from the object. For it is better for a king to be obstinate than pusillanimous and vacillating; as in the first case he might chance to be right, in the latter he is sure to be wrong. Nothing more certainly indicates the weakness of a prince than a wavering mind."

Muhammad defeated the Mughal army of Arghun Khan, king of Persia, but was himself slain in a battle against the forces of the descendant of Ghengiz Khan, who then ruled in Khorassan. He met his death, as James IV. did at Flodden, owing to a chivalrous disregard of the natural advantages of his position and a desire to fight the foe on even terms, and, like King James, he fell surrounded by the nobles of his court. The news of his death killed his father, now breaking with the burden of age and a reign of twenty-one years, and he expired in 1286.

In the reign of his grandson Keikobád, who succeeded, vice prevailed to such an extent, that every shady grove was filled with women, every street rung with riot, magistrates were seen drunk in public, and music was heard on every side. His father, Karra Khan, Viceroy of Bengal, coming to Delhi in somewhat ambiguous guise, he was compelled to kneel before his unworthy son, while the herald cried "Karra Khan comes to humble himself before the Asylum of the Universe." The father burst into tears, the son's heart was touched, and for a while he mended his ways, but those about him preferred to profit by his ruin and cast temptation in his path. One day he met a woman wearing a tiara of jewels riding an Arabian horse. A transparent robe veiled without concealing her figure and flowed loosely over her rounded shoulders, and a girdle of gems encircled her slender waist. Enraptured with her beauty, the king pitched his camp upon the fortunate foundations of the meeting-place and delivered himself over to unrestrained dissipation.

The military chiefs soon revolted. Of these, the greatest were the Khiljis, a Tartar tribe which in the tenth century had settled in Afghanistan, with which country it had long been associated and almost identified.

In 1288 Keikobád's brains were beaten out as he lay on his bed in his palace, and his body was thrown out of the window.

IV. House of Kilji (1288–1320).

The house of Kilji, which reigned at Delhi from 1288 till 1321, pretended, according to the Seljúk *nama*, to be descended from Turk, the son of Japhet, the son of Noah. However that may be, Jalál-ud-dín, the first king of that race, exhibited none of the pride of long descent, feigned extreme humility, and prostrating himself before the gate of the palace at Delhi, expressed himself unable to acknowledge the gratitude he owed to God, who had raised him so high above his compeers, many of whom were equally and even more deserving. The nobles said, "This is a strange sort of king, who has hardly placed his foot on the throne before he thinks how he shall keep it there," and, in fact, the clemency of Jalál-ud-dín was soon and often needed. First he quelled and pardoned the revolt of the nephew of Ghíyás-ud-dín; next in 1292 he repulsed the Mughals, who invaded the Punjab, 3000 of whom became converts to Islam, and the rest of whom retired unmolested across the Indus. "Evil for evil is easily returned," said the king, "but he only is great who returns good for evil. I am now old"—he was upwards of seventy—"and I wish to go down to my grave without shedding more blood." His subjects abused this clemency, and a plot to assassinate him was discovered. Jalál-ud-dín fearlessly went to the scene of the conspiracy, and finding the offenders drinking, first flung his sword upon the ground and challenged any one of them to use it against him, and when, ashamed, they declined the challenge, drank a cup of wine with them and forgave their treason. The historian narrates this circumstance, and his editor aptly remarks that it is very characteristic of the equality maintained by Muhammadans towards each other. This is a remarkable and admirable trait in the religion of Islam. Not only does the tie override all race distinction, but in some sense it obliterates social differences. Master and servant will travel together, mess together, and pray together on a footing of equality *sans gêne*, and yet preserve in all essentials and in all necessary aspects the respect due from each to the other.

One of the most remarkable characters of this reign was Sidi Mowla, a dervish of Delhi, who daily expended large sums in feeding the poor, and acquired great influence in the city. His success in the part of philosopher and mendicant inspired him with ambition, and he plotted the assassination of the king, who ordered him to undergo the ordeal of fire. The ministers advised, however, that it was the nature of fire to consume the innocent and guilty alike, and Jalál-ud-dín remarked to some religious mendicants by his side, "I leave the sinner to be dealt with according to his deserts." On this one of the mendicants began to cut Sidi Mowla's throat with a razor, in the informal way in which executions were till quite recently conducted in Persia. The sufferer, with Oriental submission to fate, made no resistance, but addressing the king said, "I am glad you have decided to slay me at once, but my curse will lie heavy upon you and your posterity." The execution was then completed by an elephant, who trampled upon Sidi Mowla till he died.

As if to accomplish the holy man's curse, troubles began to gather around the head of Jalál-ud-dín, and his eldest son died. His nephew, Alá-ud-dín, however, put down insurrections in Bandelkand and Malwa, and for the first time in 1294 led a Muhammadan force into the Dekhan, marching from Karrah, near Allahabad, across the Vindhya mountains to Deogiri or Daulatábád, the capital of Ram Deo, the king of the Maráthá country, took the fort, and returned after an absence of one year, the Hindu Raja having ceded Ellichpur and paid an enormous ransom in gold and precious stones.

The councillors of Jalál-ud-dín feared the fortunes, and advised him to protect himself against the overweening ambition, of his nephew. The king, however, confident in the loyalty of Alá-ud-dín, met him privately and without any suspicion of treachery, and raising him from the ground, protested that he disbelieved the representations of his enemies, and held him dearer than his own offspring. At this moment the perfidious nephew beckoned to assassins, who cut off the monarch's head, fixed it on the point of a spear, and carried it through camp and city. Thus died Jalál-ud-dín Khilji in 1295, when Alá-ud-dín ascended to the throne of Hindustan over the body of his uncle and benefactor to enjoy a long and glorious reign. In 1297 he completed the conquest of Gujarat, and defeated a great invasion of the Mughals under Kutlugh Khan, the general of the king of Transoxiana, whose army is said to have consisted of 200,000 horse. The battle was fought near Delhi, and in it the great chief Zafar Khan fell, exclaiming to the Mughal who offered him his life and honour, "I know no greater honour than to die in fulfilling my duty." After this victory Alá-ud-dín, puffed up with pride, began to entertain the projects of establishing a new religion and of conquering the world like Alexander. From these he was diverted by a Moslem sage, who reminded him that Muhammad was the last of the prophets; that he had no counsellor like Aristotle, and could not depend, as Alexander did, upon the affection of his people; and that if he thirsted for glory, he should gain it by subduing the Hindu princes of Central and Southern India, and by protecting India against the invasions of the Mughals.

Taking this excellent advice in good part, the king set

to work to reduce the fortress of Rintimbur, when his life was attempted by his nephew, who had learnt too well the lesson he himself had taught. Rintimbur fell in 1300, and three years later he took Chitor, the seat of the chief of the Rajput princes, and in 1304 and 1305 was occupied in repelling several invasions of Mughals.

Vexed by continual revolts and conspiracies, the king called together his nobles, and asked them to advise as to the causes and the cure of the evils that beset the state. He was frankly told that not the least of the causes were his inattention to business, his devotion to wine, the unequal division of property, and the too close connections formed between the royal family and the chief officers of the court. The king thereon applied himself vigorously to the administration of justice, and so urgently did he insist on temperance, that he ordered all the wine in Delhi to be emptied into the streets. This may occasionally be seen to this day in Persia, when an outbreak of religious enthusiasm prompts the Muslim governor to be orthodox at the expense of the Armenian wine merchant. He enforced the punctual payment of the land-tax of 50 per cent. of the gross annual produce. The proportion actually taken by the British Government, it may be remarked in passing, very rarely exceeds 20, and is generally considerably under 20 per cent.; in the case of unirrigated land varying from 5 to 10 per cent. The English, however, fixed the assessment in money, whereas the Muhammadans merely commuted the Hindu payment in grain into a money payment, which varied according to value of produce and of the precious metals. At each step the tax, though lighter in incidence, is collected and enforced in a manner less suitable to the conditions of an agricultural people. Alá-ud-dín fulfilled the law of Islam in exacting tribute from the Hindus to the uttermost farthing, so that the punishment might approximate as nearly as possible to death, for the law said, "Tax them to the extent they can pay, or utterly destroy them." He held, on the advice of his law-officers, that if a public servant, who was sufficiently paid, took bribes, it was lawful to recover the money by rack or torture. He fixed the prices of horses, arms, and provisions of all kinds throughout Hindustan. Two pounds of unhusked rice were sold for 30 dwts. of copper, good horses for 160, and ponies for 20 rupees. Ordinary country ponies now cost from 80 to 160 rupees. A price was fixed for everything, down to the favours of the public women, who were divided into three classes. Ridiculous as many of his measures were, Alá-ud-dín was not only a great conqueror, but he enforced law and order with a hand of iron throughout his extensive dominions. He held that "the will of a wise prince is better than the opinions of variable bodies of men"; that a good tyrant may be "freedom's best and truest friend."

After his general, Shaz Beg Tughlak, had repulsed the inroads of the Mughals in 1304 and 1305, Alá-ud-dín despatched an army against Warangal in the Dekhan, and sent a large force under Málik Káfur to reduce the Raja of Deogiri, who had ceased to pay tribute, while the Muhammadan king was occupied with other foes in the north. Málik Káfur was successful in his operations in the Dekhan. In this campaign the daughter of the Raja of Gujarat, a maiden of surpassing beauty, was captured, and became the bride of Alá-ud-dín's son, Khizr Khan. In 1310 another expedition was despatched to subdue the western coast, from the site of the modern city of Bombay, southwards, and the uplands of Satára and Bijapur. Málik Káfur returned in 1311 with a prodigious treasure of gold and precious stones. No mention is made of silver, and Ferishta expressly says that no person wore bracelets, chains, or rings of any other metal than gold, of which material, also, was fashioned the plate in the houses of the rich and in the temples of the gods. In fact, as in the times of King Solomon, and indeed in later times, "silver was nothing accounted of."

After the conquest of the Dekhan, the king gave himself up to pride and passion, and in 1311 massacred 15,000 Mughals in Delhi, because he had discovered a plot by one of that race to assassinate him. His prosperity began to decline, and the power of the eunuch Málik Káfur increased daily, to the disgust of the nobles and the people. The minister poisoned the mind of Alá-ud-dín against the members of his own family, and the flames of rebellion had burst forth in Gujarat and elsewhere, when the king suddenly died in 1316, after a reign of twenty years, during which his power and wealth surpassed that of any prince who had sat on the throne of Hindustan.

After a year of disorder and assassination, Mubárik Khilji ascended a blood-stained throne. To obtain popularity, and possibly from some feeling of clemency, he released 17,000 prisoners, and gave six months' pay to all the troops. But the promotion of a renegade Hindu to the office of vizier gave great offence, especially as, before his conversion to Islam, he had belonged to one of the lowest of castes. In 1318 he marched to Deogiri in the Dekhan, and taking Harpal Deo, son-in-law of Ram Deo, prisoner, flayed him alive, decapitated him, and fixed his head upon the gate—a proceeding as barbarous as that of the Covenanters who put Montrose to death in Scotland at a later date. The king's debauchery equalled his cruelty. He used to dress like an actress and dance at the houses of the nobility, and caused obscene representations to be performed by women of loose character before the court. Meanwhile, Málik Khusrú, his general, conquered Malabar in 1319, and presently assassinated his master. A donative to the household troops confirmed the usurper for a while upon the throne, but Ghazi Khan Tughlak, governor of the Punjab, marched upon Delhi, declaring that he had but unsheathed his sword to deliver the people from the oppressor of whom he had rid the world, and he sought in vain for a member of the family of Alá-ud-dín, for all had been slain. So the successful general became king himself, as has often happened before and since down to the days of Napoleon, and he ascended the throne as Ghíyás-ud-dín Tughlak in 1321. This family ruled in Delhi from the days of Edward II. till the accession of Henry V. of England.

V. House of Tughlak (1321–1414).

It is stated by Ferishta that Ghíyás-ud-dín was the son of a Turki slave of Ghíyás-ud-dín Balban by a Jat or Punjábi mother. He successfully fortified his frontier against the Mughals, and his son proceeded in 1322 to settle the Dekhan, and after some initial reverses captured Warangal and reduced the Telingána country. The king himself confirmed Bakarra Khan in the government of Bengal, and reduced Tirhut, the classical Mithila. On his return to Delhi he was received by his son in a wooden pavilion, which, either by design or accident, fell upon him and crushed him to death. God alone, as the Muhammadan historian says, knows the truth of this matter, but the son who raised the structure was, by its fall, raised to the throne of the deceased monarch by the title of Muhammad Tughlak in 1323. He commenced his reign by acts of largesse and liberality, by patronising men of letters, and by acquiring a knowledge of letters himself. He wrote well in Arabic and Persian was skilled in physic, logic, astronomy, mathematics, and medicine, never neglected his religious duties, and abstained from all vices forbidden in the Koran. None the less was he wholly devoid of the divine quality of mercy, though distinguished for bravery and gallantry in the field.

In 1327 the Mughals subdued Multan and the surrounding country, and Muhammad Tughlak bought them off as they marched towards Delhi, and then proceeded to reduce the Dekhan, which was ever in revolt, to obedience, and to conquer the Carnatic, and to engage in mad schemes for the conquest of Persia, Nipal, and China. To provide funds for his extravagant projects he increased taxation, tampered with the coinage, repudiated his debts, and became involved in inextricable confusion. So little was he affected by the misery he had caused, that he ordered the wholesale removal of all the inhabitants of Delhi to Deogiri or Daulatábad. Twice he enforced this inhuman order, and on one occasion he called out his army to hunt the miserable peasants, who, owing to his exactions, had ceased to cultivate the fertile land between the Ganges and the Jumna. The Viceroy of the Punjab now rebelled, but was taken and slain; the king's nephew in Malwa raised the standard of revolt; Bengal and the Carnatic revolted, and were lost to the empire, and the Afghans and the Ghakkars ravaged the north-west frontier.

The Hindu Rajas of the Telingána and the Carnatic seized the opportunity to recover their independence in 1344, and to establish themselves respectively at Warangal and at Vijáyanagar, the desolate ruins of which on the solitary banks of the Tungabadra give mournful evidence of its former greatness. From this date forward till the end of the sixteenth century, however, the kingdom of Vijáyaganar held its own against the Muhammadans in the Dekhan.

In 1345 a famine raged in Hindustan, and the governors of Malwa and Gujarat revolted. But in the Dekhan the king's son-in-law, Imád-ul-Mulk was slain by Hasan Ganga, who founded the Báhmani dynasty, and the whole country was lost to the empire. Muhammad proceeded first to subdue the revolt in Gujarat, but while so engaged died at Tatta, on the delta of the Indus, in 1351, from the effects of a surfeit of fish.

During this reign many Mughals in India became converts to Islam and entered the service of the king of Delhi.

Ibn Batuta, a native of Tangiers, who visited Delhi in 1341, has given an account of the city during the reign of Muhammad, and has dwelt with equal force upon its beauty and its desolate condition, filled with mosques and palaces, but bereft of any proportionate complement of inhabitants. Ibn Batuta says he was received with kindness by the king, and his wants were so carefully considered that a special stipend was allowed by the state for his washing. But why not? for in these days the Government of India allots a stipend for the upkeep of the cat which eats the rats which might devour the records. The prime minister attended the funeral of the traveller's daughter, and the king made him a judge, and despatched him upon an embassy to China. Muhammad, as a great prince, had diplomatic relations with his neighbours. He solicited investiture from the Caliph in Egypt, and entertained his envoy, and he gave asylum to a prince of the house of Abbas. The revenue of the Dekhan was at this time computed to be £1,166,000; but it is very doubtful if in any year so great a revenue found its way into the Moslem coffers. Posts on horseback, such as are described in the Book of Esther, and such as exist to this day in Persia, were established from end to end of the wide dominions of Muhammad, which in India at the commencement of his reign exceeded those of any previous king of Hindustan. Few monarchs have left behind such a reputation for the possession of talents which were a curse to themselves and their subjects. This monster, however, was not without a sense of humour, and when a learned doctor of the law remonstrated with him for the indiscriminate infliction of the punishment of death, and enumerated the few offences for which the extreme penalty is allowed by the Koran, he replied, "All that may be very true; but mankind has become much worse since those laws were made." In the same way it is humorously urged sometimes that champagne is not forbidden to the believer, for it had not been invented when the book was written.

Firuz Tughlak, the cousin of Muhammad, succeeded him, and spent the first year or two of his reign in trying to recover Bengal, the independence of which province and of the Dekhan he was, however, constrained to recognise in 1356; and after years of successive revolt and submission by different provinces of the empire he died at the age of ninety in 1388, having allowed the actual power to be exercised by his vizier for some years before his decease. Firuz built the city of Firuzabad, adjacent to Delhi, and constructed several public works of great utility. He limited the number of offences for which death was the punishment; fixed the revenue demands so as to leave little scope for the extortions of collectors; and abolished the practice of mutilation, though it is expressly permitted by the Muhammadan law. The fame of his useful reign reached Cairo, and the Caliph sent him an honorary dress and a letter of congratulation in 1356. The greatest of Firuz's works was a canal from Karṇal, near the great battlefield of Panipat, upon the Jumna, to Hansi and Husár, on the border of the desert of Bikanir, which still serves its original purpose, and is maintained by the British Government for irrigation. The character of Firuz can best be gathered from the records he has left behind him, a translation of one of which, preserved by Ferishta, is worthy of reproduction even in a brief history of the Muhammadan epoch.

"It has been usual in former times to spill Muhammadan blood on trivial occasions, and for small crimes to mutilate and torture them, by cutting off the hands and feet, and noses and ears, by putting out eyes, by pulverising the bones of the living criminal with mallets, by burning the body with fire, by crucifixion, and by nailing the hands and feet, by flaying alive, by the operation of ham-stringing, and by cutting human beings to pieces. God in His infinite goodness, having been pleased to confer on me the power, has also inspired me with the disposition to put an end to these practices. It is my resolution, moreover, to restore, in the daily prayers offered up for the royal family, the names of all those princes, my predecessors, who have reigned over the empire of Delhi, in hopes that these prayers, being acceptable to God, may in some measure appease His wrath, and ensure His mercy towards them. It is also hereby proclaimed that the small and vexatious taxes payable to the public servants of Government as perquisites of offices by small traders; that licenses for the right of pasturage from shepherds on waste lands belonging to the crown; fees from flower-sellers, fish-sellers, cotton-cleaners, and cooks; and the precarious and fluctuating taxes on shopkeepers and vintners, shall henceforth cease throughout the realm; for it is better to relinquish this portion of the revenue than realise it at the expense of so much distress, occasioned by the discretionary power necessarily vested in tax-gatherers and officers of authority; nor will any tax hereafter be levied contrary to the written law of the book. It has been customary to set aside one-fifth of all property taken in war for the troops, and to reserve four-fifths to the Government. It is hereby ordered that in future four-fifths shall be distributed to the troops, and one-fifth only reserved for the Crown. I will on all occasions cause to be banished from the realm persons convicted of the following crimes:—Those who profess atheism, or who maintain schools of vice; all public servants convicted of corruption, as well as persons paying bribes. I have myself abstained from wearing gaudy silk apparel and jewels, as an example to my subjects. I have considered it my duty to repair every public edifice of utility constructed by my predecessors—such as caravanseras, musjids, wells, reservoirs of water, aqueducts, canals, hospitals, almshouses, and schools, and have alienated considerable portions of the revenue for their support. I have also taken pains to discover the surviving relations of all persons who suffered from the wrath of my late lord and master, Muhammad Toghlak, and having pensioned and provided for them, have caused them to grant their full pardon and forgiveness to that prince, in presence of the holy and learned men of this age, whose signatures and seals as witnesses are affixed to the documents, the whole of which, as far as lay in my power, have been procured and put into a box, and deposited in the vault in which Muhammad Toghlak is entombed. I have gone and sought consolation from all the most learned and holy men within my realm, and have taken care of them. Whenever my soldiers have been rendered inefficient for service by wounds or by age, I have caused them to be pensioned on full pay for life. Two attempts have been made to poison me, but without effect."

Ghíyás-ud-dín Tughlak II. reigned but a few months,

and was succeeded by Abubakr, a grandson of Firuz, in whose time and in that of his successor, Násir-ud-dín, the Hindu-born Muhammadans and the Hindus continued to acquire strength and importance.

VI. Tamerlane and Anarchy (1398–1414).

Mahmúd, son of Násir-ud-dín, assumed the style of king in 1394, and presently lost Gujarat, Malwa, and Khándesh, the governors of which provinces asserted their independence; and intestine strife prevailed in Hindustan, when, in 1398, the storm burst, and the fitful inroads of the Mughals culminated in the desolating invasion of Tamerlane.

Like Ghengiz Khan, nearly 200 years earlier, Timur the Lame had collected under his sway the tribes of Tartary. He himself had been born near Samarkand, and pretended to be of the same stock as Ghengiz. Timur, however, was a Turk and a Mussulman, and he had conquered Persia and Transoxiana, and had invaded Georgia and Mesopotamia, and parts of Russia and Siberia, before he turned his attention to India. Ghengiz Khan was Mongol, belonging to the smallest branch of the four great divisions of the Tartars, and his armies had been composed chiefly of Turks, the most widely extended of those four divisions, and it has been briefly narrated how he took Pekin and annexed the northern provinces of China, subdued Kharizm—the king of which reigned from the Persian Gulf to the borders of India and Turkestan—took Transoxiana and Khorassan, overthrew all the independent kingdoms of Tartary, and died in the fulness of glory in 1227.

Octai, his son, succeeded as great Khan of the Mongols and Tartars; and after him came his son Gayuk, and the grandsons of Ghengiz, Mangon and Kublai Khan. Between 1227 and 1295 they conquered all China, and reduced to varying degrees of obedience Corea, Tonkin, Cochin-China, Pegu, Bengal, and Thibet, and in vain attempted the conquest of Japan. Holakou, the brother of Kublai, conquered Persia, and expelled the Assassains from their fastnesses near Kazveen, and deposed Mostasem, the last of the Caliphs of Bagdad, in 1258, and the victorious Mongols plundered Aleppo and Damascus, and had subverted Egypt too, but for the fact that the softer inhabitants of the Nile valley were defended by the hardy Mamluks. The last of the Seljukian Sultans of Iconium disappeared before their conquering hordes. Batou, the nephew of Octai, traversed the plains of Kipchak with a great army, destroyed Moscow and Kieff, and settled permanently in Russia, whence his troops overwhelmed Cracow, and defeated the Dukes of Silesia and the Polish princes at Legnitz, and invaded Hungary. The King Bela in vain endeavoured to oppose the invaders, and all north of the Danube was prostrate before the Mongols, who retired northwards in 1245, after wasting Servia, Bosnia, and Bulgaria. The brother of Batou entered Siberia, and his descendants reigned in that country for three centuries, till the Russian conquest.

The great Khan Kublai held his court at Pekin, whence 150 years later his dynasty was expelled by the Chinese, after the conquerors had, however, become for the most part merged among the Chinese. The conquered parts of Russia, Kipchak, Transoxiana, and Persia became independent of the great Khan, and under their respective kings adopted the religion of Islam, and ceased to have any communication with the Mughals proper.

Meanwhile, of the Turkoman hordes which had fought under the Sultan of Kharizm, who returned after his defeat by Ghengiz to recover his kingdom, some upon his death invaded Syria, and others entered the service of the Sultan of Iconium. These tribes had originally been located upon the southern bank of the Oxus, and from them issued one Orthogrul, the son of Soliman, the father of Othman or Osman, the founder of the Ottomans or Osmanlis, who took Boursa from the Greek Emperor and subdued Bithynia up to the shores of the Propontis. In the domestic rivalry between the Cantacuzeni and the Palæologi for the throne of Constantinople, Soliman, the son of Orchan, the son of Othman, was called in by the former prince, and out-staying his welcome, settled in Thrace in 1353. Amurath I., son of Orchan, subdued the whole of that province up to the walls of Constantinople and made Adrianople the seat of his government, destroyed the power of the Slav principalities, and made thousands of his European captives Moslems and members of his bodyguard, the origin of the famous force of the Janizaries. Amurath's successor, Bajazet or Ilderim, who ascended the throne in 1389, reduced all Anatolia, brought the Servians and Bulgarians under the yoke, and Macedonia and Thessaly, received the title of Sultan from the Caliph at Cairo, and defeated Sigismond, king of Hungary, at Nicopolis in 1396. Constantinople would have now fallen into the hands of the Ottomans had not Bajazet been defeated by Tamerlane in 1402.

Timur is commonly described as a Mongul or Mughal, because he claimed to be the representative of Ghengiz Khan and because he revived the Tartar Empire. He defended Transoxiana against the kings of Kashgar, with such success that in 1370 he received the chief command, and between that date and 1400 annexed Kharizm and Persia, which for half a century, since the death of the last ruler of the house of Ghengiz, had been a prey to intestine strife, and reduced Turkestan or Eastern Tartary and Kipchak or Western Tartary to obedience, and from Kipchak invaded Russia and took the Duke of Moscow prisoner. From the invasion of India in 1398, of which more detailed notice is necessary here, he was turned by the news of revolts in Anatolia and Georgia, which had lately embraced the religion, when smitten by the sword, of the conqueror. At the age of sixty-three he marched from Samarcand to Georgia, and thence to Syria, where he took Aleppo and Damascus from the Circassian Mamluks, who had deposed the Turkish kings. He then collected all his strength for the defeat of the Ottoman Sultan Bajazet in 1402 at Angora, on the borders of Anatolia. Smyrna alone of the towns of Asia Minor offered any real resistance to Tamerlane, who, however, finally took it, and put all the Christians, including the Knights of Rhodes, the valiant defenders of the city, to the sword. Death arrested his career of conquest as he marched towards China in 1405. Within a hundred years from his death Persia and Transoxiana were overrun by nomad Turkmans, and his descendant Bábar, flying from the Uzbegs, founded the Mughal Empire in India, while the Ottoman Empire, secured against invasion from the east, consolidated its strength in Asia Minor and in Europe under Amurath II.

To return to India: Tamerlane entered that country by way of Kabul, after sending his grandson before him to ravage the territory around Multan, and marching across the rivers of the Punjab, on reaching Delhi, put to death 100,000 prisoners who had been taken captive on the way, and on December 17, 1398, entered Delhi, whence Mahmúd Tughlak had fled, and was proclaimed Emperor of India. It is related that he stationed in his entrenchments a line of buffaloes facing the enemy, whether in the hope that the Hindus would not run the risk of slaying these animals or not, is uncertain.

It would be interesting to discover if the barbarian knew of the Egyptian army which refused to engage the enemy to whose shields were tied the cats. It does appear certain that little resistance was offered to the troops of Tamerlane, who proceeded to regulate the contributions of the inhabitants to his army. The wealthier inhabitants proving unwilling to pay their share of the indemnity, the troops were admitted, and a dreadful massacre ensued, followed by a wholesale loot. "The desperate courage of the Delhians," says Ferishta, "was cooled in their own blood, and throwing down their weapons, they at last submitted themselves like sheep to the slaughter." The city had surrendered under promise of protection, but it is doubtful how far this merciless slaughter resulted from a perfidious disregard of engagements, and how far from inability to restrain a victorious army of barbarians.

After feasting and rejoicing, while the miserable inhabitants of Delhi were for five days the victims of fire and sword, Tamerlane offered up to God "a sincere and humble tribute of grateful praise" in the mosque built by Firoz Tughlak on the banks of the Jumna, and quitted India, regardless of the disorganised condition in which he left it, to prosecute the war against the Ottoman Sultan. From his own memoirs this destroying prince seems to have combined in his own person a strange mixture of the bold and simple soldier with the wily and scheming politician. His personal bravery was conspicuous, and he habitually exposed his own person like that of a private soldier.

In 1405 Mahmúd returned to Delhi, which in the interval had been the prey of anarchy and usurpation, and in 1414 he died.

VII. The Sayyids (1414–1450).

Khizr Khan, governor of the Punjab, then assumed the government, nominally as the lieutenant of Tamerlane. As he was a descendant of the Prophet, he and his family are generally known as the dynasty of the Sayyids, and they remained in authority, practically within the walls of Delhi only, till 1450, when Behlól Khan Lódí assumed the title of king, after the troubled reign of Sayyid Mubarik, a prince of energy and decision of character, of whom it is recorded that he possessed so equal a temper, that it was notorious that he never spoke in anger to any person during his troubled life, which was terminated by the hand of a Hindu assassin while he prayed within the mosque. The reigns of the Sayyids Muhammad and Alá-ud-dín call for little notice.

VIII. The Lodis (1450–1526).

When Behlól Lódí ascended the throne, the Dekhan, Gujarat, Malwa, and Bengal each had an independent king, while the Punjab and Sirhind had been governed by himself, so that his accession reunited these territories to Delhi. Behlól was the grandson of a governor of Multan under Firoz Tughlak and an Afghan by birth, of a family which had originally carried on trade between Persia and India. He waged a successful war against the king of Juanpur, whose territory surrounded the town of Benares, and on his death in 1488 the kingdom of Delhi extended from the Jumna to the Himálayas and from the capital to Benares. He was a virtuous prince, of such humility that he seldom sat upon the throne, saying that it was enough for him that the world knew he was king, without any display of authority. Sikandar Lódí, a son of Behlól, succeeded, and he reannexed Bihár and Bandelkand to the crown of Delhi. He was a good administrator, but a bigot, of whom it is recorded that he put a Brahman to death for holding that "all religions, if sincerely practised, were equally acceptable to God."

As French history records the oath of the racquet-court, the annals of the Lódis relate the conspiracy of the poló-ground, which resulted from one player having struck another with his stick during the progress of the game. During this reign a calamitous earthquake occurred at Agra. Sikandar was remarkable for the beauty of his person, and for his devotion to business and to religion. He practised and encouraged charity. One day when he was marching to battle a calendar prayed for his victory; he replied, "Pray rather that victory may be his who will best promote the good of his subjects." Gibbon, however, ascribes this lofty sentiment to Málik Shah, son of the Sultan Alp Arslán.

Ibráhím Lódí succeeded to the throne, but not to the virtues, of his father. His reign was disturbed by rebellions, but lasted from 1517 till 1526. Of the reigns of Sikandar and Ibráhím no very accurate accounts have come down to us; but the years between 1488 and 1526 saw the end of the dominion of the Moors in Spain in 1491, the discovery of America by Columbus in 1494, the arrival of the Portuguese in India by way of the Cape of Good Hope, the accession of Henry VIII. to the throne of England, the conquest of Mexico by Cortez, and the circumnavigation of the globe by Magellan in 1522. We know little of Indian history in this pregnant period.

Ibráhím's precarious tenure of power ended with the invasion of Bábar, the first of the great Mughals. Daulat Khan Lódí, governor of the Punjab, called in the aid of Bábar, who was then reigning in Kábul, and who had already invaded the Punjab, claiming that country as the inheritance of Tamerlane. Bábar first sacked and destroyed Lahore in 1524, and then returned to Kabul, whence in 1526 he again returned to India, and gave battle to Ibráhím Lódí at Pánípat. The latter prince had an army of 100,000 men and 1000 elephants, and the former but 12,000 men; but the Indians were routed and Ibráhím slain. Bábar then occupied Delhi and Agra, and, to use the words of Elphinstone, "founded a line of kings under whom India rose to the highest pitch of prosperity, and out of the ruins of whose empire all the existing states in that country are composed."

Meanwhile the necessities of a comparative treatment of the subject require a brief reference to the progress of the Muhammadans on both sides of the Hellespont, in Europe and in Asia. The Ottoman Sultan Amurath II., in a long and glorious reign, 1421–1451, witnessed the temporary union of the emperors of Constantinople with the popes of Rome, and the efforts of the former and the latter combined to make head against his victorious house, and the reunion of the Greek and Latin Churches, whose religious differences were absorbed for a season in a common dread of the Turk. At the bidding of the Pope, and from motives of interest and self-preservation, the Hungarians and Poles, under Ladislaus and John Hunyades, combined against the common enemy, and, crossing the Danube, reached Sophia, and concluded a truce of ten years with Amurath. To the disgrace of the Christians this treaty was perfidiously broken when it appeared that Amurath was weakened by domestic rebellions. The Sultan none the less defeated Ladislaus at Varna in 1444, and in 1453 his son Muhammad II. defeated the Greeks, took Constantinople, and trampled under foot the religion that there had not taught its professors to keep their solemn promises for any longer time than suited their political purposes. A war was declared at the Diet of Frankfort in 1454, but no actual steps were taken against the Turk. In 1459 the Pope convened an European congress at Mantua, but its great promise bore no fruit in performance, while the Ottomans recruited their armies by a tax of every fifth male child born to its Christian population, when the recruitment of captives from Bulgaria, Servia, and Albania had ceased. In 1480 Muhammad took Otranto, but speedily relinquished this solitary conquest in Italy, and on his death in the following year a disputed possession and domestic troubles suspended the career of Ottoman conquest.

CHAPTER IV.

THE HOUSE OF TIMUR THE MUGHAL (1526-1857).

I. BÁBAR (1526–1530).

THE Padshah Bábar, to give him the title usually adopted by the emperors of his line, has fortunately left behind him memoirs in the Turki language of his adventurous career, of which all writers on Indian history have availed themselves. His career lasted from 1482–1530, and he was the contemporary of Henry VII. and Henry VIII. of England. He lived but four years after the conquest of Delhi, of which he was king from 1526–1530 only. His father was the fifth in descent from Tamerlane, who, as has been stated, was a Turk by descent. The father, on the partition of the dominions of his father, Abu Said, had obtained the little kingdom of Ferghana, on the Jaxartes. His mother was a Mughal, but throughout his memoirs Bábar speaks with contempt and dislike of the race, by the name of which the Indians have erroneously called his dynasty. Mughal is a generic term with them for a Muhammadan who enters India from beyond Afghanistan. In 1497 Bábar took Samarkand. "I was but fifteen at that time," says he, "and had seen little service. I took the city and put the king to flight. I do not intend by this to extol my own actions; but in writing a history of my military career, it is proper I should state things as they really occurred." After a reign in the City of Safety of a hundred days he was recalled to Ferghana by a revolt; and when in 1499 he had re-established himself in his patrimony, he learnt that the Uzbeks, a mass of Turki and Mughal tribes united as one people, and called after one of their khans, had taken Samarkand and Bokhara, which they continued to possess until the recent conquest of the Russians. For some years the future Padshah of India, "the football of fortune, like a king on a chess-board, moved from place to place, and, buffeted about like a pebble on the sea-shore, sought the help and advice of his neighbours." After many adventures, in his twenty-third year he determined to seek his fortunes across the Hindu Kush, in command of an army of Mughals from Balkh, which voluntarily entered into his service. With these troops he invaded Kábul, which had fallen into the hands of a Mughal who had dispossessed his own uncle. In 1504 he occupied the present capital of Afghanistan, and losing Balkh, which was occupied by the Uzbeks, he became king of Kábul, and reigned there for twenty-two years before he invaded India, in continual warfare with the mountain tribes of Afghanistan, then, as now, well-nigh indomitable, and in opposing his formidable neighbours the Uzbeks. In 1508 he was temporarily dispossessed from his government by a Mughal insurrection, and for some years he was harassed by Shaibání Khan of the Uzbeks, who took Herat and Kandahar, but was, providentially for Bábar, defeated and slain by Shah Ismail Saffavi of Persia in 1510. In 1514, after brief successes, he suffered a crushing defeat at the hands of the Uzbeks, after which he finally turned his attention from the country north of the Hindu Kush to India.

After his victory at Pánípat, Bábar had still to make good his footing in the country. He compares his successes with those of Mahmúd of Ghazni and Muhammad Ghorí, and says how small were his resources compared with theirs. He did not ascribe his victory to his own exertions, but to the favour of the Almighty, who was pleased to aid his efforts. The first of his troubles was the discontent of his troops with the Indian climate; but the Padshah expressed his own intention of remaining, whereupon most of his chiefs resolved to stay, and before long all the Muhammadan princes in India acknowledged his supremacy. But the Rajput kings of Chitor and Mewat, with other Hindu princes, now resolved to expel the new invader and marched to Fatehpur Síkri, near Agra, to give battle to the Muhammadans. The adverse prediction of an astrologer produced a despondent feeling in the minds of Bábar's chiefs and soldiers, but he made an appeal to their honour, and for his own part cheerfully engaged the enemy and gained a great victory. His triumph was the greater that his advisers had counselled returning to Kábul, to which Bábar replied, "What will the Muhammadan kings of the world say of a monarch whom the fear of death obliged to abandon such a kingdom? It is more consistent with true heroism to reconcile ourselves to martyrdom; for as it is certain that the soul must quit the body, it is fit that it should do so with honour, for the whole object of a man's life should be that when he dies he may leave behind him a spotless name." In fact, Bábar thought the purple a worthy mantle for a monarch living, and a glorious shroud for the dead.

After the defeat of the Raja of Mewat, he reduced his country, and laid siege to Chándéri, the Rajput garrison of which fortress put their women to death and rushed forth naked to immolate themselves upon the swords of the Muslims; and he took Rintimbur, a famous fortress near Ajmír, and reduced Bihár to obedience. Though the latter province was subsequently seized by Mahmúd

Lódí for a season, Bábar soon recovered it, and added also to his possessions the portion of that kingdom lying north of the Ganges. Bábar died at Agra in 1530, and was buried at Kábul. In person he was handsome, in address engaging and unaffected, and in disposition amiable and affectionate. His own style was plain and manly, like that of his writings. In domestic life he was as admirable as in war he was brave. He records in his letters that the scent of a melon from Kábul brought tears to his eyes, when he thought of his exile from his native land. Though a warrior above all things, he loved wine and women, and to lie reclined in walled gardens by bubbling brooks. He fully realised the ideal of the great Persian poet in the lines which may thus most inadequately be translated—

> "Cup-bearer mine, pour out the wine, pause not while life is ours,
> For when we die, inert we lie, no more in rosy bowers,
> By limpid rill, we drink our fill, and crown the cup with flowers."

In a grove near Kábul he used to fill a reservoir with wine, when he had a mind to make merry. In the words of Elphinstone, "he was the most admirable, though not the most powerful, prince that ever reigned in Asia."

II. HUMÁYÚN (1530–1556) AND SHER SHAH THE AFGHAN (1540–1555).

Humáyún, who succeeded Bábar, was a prince of wit and urbanity, fond of pleasure, but devoted none the less to astronomy and geography. He had three brothers, Kámrán, Hindal, and Mirza Askari. The first named was governor of Kábul and Kandahar, and possessed the support and attachment of those who had been far longer subject to the family of Bábar than had the

Hindus. Humáyún gave up to Kámrán the Punjab, and appointed his other brothers to governments in India.

Fortunately for future ages, Abul Fazl, the great minister of Akbar, and Joher, a servant of Humáyún, have both left memoirs dealing with this reign, in which its most important events have been recorded.

At the commencement of his reign Humáyún had to deal with rebellions of Afghan chiefs, who hated the new Muhammadan invaders more than the Hindus, and with the opposition of Bahádur Shah, king of Gujarat, which kingdom had risen to independence and importance upon the dissolution of the empire of Delhi. The Padshah marched against his enemy in 1534, the momentous year which saw the Protestant religion established in England, and from a chivalrous regard for the position of a Mussalman who was engaged in making war against the infidel Hindus, waited till Bahádur had taken Chitor, and then attacked and defeated his army, the artillery of which was commanded by a Turkish officer from Constantinople, and pursued him to Cambay, upon the coast, where, it is recorded, a forest tribe raided upon the imperial camp, and, among other valuables, carried off the Emperor's copy of the history of Tamerlane.

Bahádur Shah escaped, and Humáyún sat down before the strong fort of Chámpanir, which he took in 1535 by assault, 300 men, of whom the Padshah was one, having fixed steel spikes in the scarp of the rock. The Raja's treasure was hidden here, and the officer in charge declining to state the locality where it was buried, was about to be tortured, when Humáyún said that wine would more pleasantly and as efficaciously unlock his lips; and when he had babbled forth the necessary particulars in his cups, a vast treasure was discovered beneath a reservoir. Humáyún soon had occasion to leave Gujarat, which was then recovered by Bahádur

Shah, to oppose Sher Khan, an Afghan noble who had been intrusted by Bábar with the government of Bíhar, and who in 1537 was also possessed of the strong fortresses of Chanár and Rotás, south and south-east of Benares, and had occupied no small portion of Bengal, with the king of which country, Mahmúd, he was at war when Humáyún marched against him. The possession of Chanár proved of immense advantage to Sher Khan, who strongly garrisoned that fort, which delayed Humáyún several months upon his march, while his artful rival completed the conquest of Bengal by defeating Mahmúd and taking Gaur, upon the left bank of the Ganges, then the capital of the kingdom. From Chanár the onward march of Humáyún was not opposed by Sher Khan, who allowed him unopposed to occupy Gaur, while he himself removed to the fortress of Rotás, there to abide throughout the long period of the rains, while Humáyún's army, cut off from its base and unoccupied, suffered severely from sickness, idleness, and fever. Immediately the rains ceased, Sher Khan recovered Chanár, and cut off all communication with Upper India; notwithstanding which the Padshah determined to force his way through to Agra, in the effort to accomplish which object he was routed, first at Monghir, and subsequently near Baxár, when the imperial army was attacked in front and rear, surprised and routed, and Humáyún was obliged to swim the Ganges on horseback. His horse was lost, and he had hardly escaped but for the assistance afforded by one of the inflated ski[illegible] in which Indian watermen carry water. In 1539 Humáyún returned a fugitive to Agra, his army reduced by war and sickness to a pitiful fraction of what it had been. The proud spirit of the Padshah could ill brook so great a reverse, and in the following year he marched to Kanouj, situated upon the Ganges north of Cawnpur, to which place Sher Khan had advanced, and was there defeated and driven into the Ganges, which he crossed upon the back of an elephant, and, on reaching the other side, he was pulled up the slippery bank by a rope of turbans. He fled to Agra, which was now untenable, and thence to Lahore, the seat of his brother Kámrán, who, however, gave up the Punjab to Sher Khan and retreated to Kábul, when Humáyún fled to Sindh with a few followers, in the hope that that province would support him. He was, however, soon bereft of men and money, and threw himself upon the protection of the Raja of Marwar. When that prince declined to help him, he fled towards Umarkot, one of his followers refusing to exchange his own fresh, for the fugitive Emperor's exhausted, horse. He and his followers suffered terribly from want of water, and from over-indulgence when, after three days' thirst, a well was found. At last, with only seven attendants, the hapless Mughal reached Umarkot, where his queen gave birth, in October 1542, to the illustrious Akbar, destined to be the greatest king of his house, and the greatest prince that ever reigned in India. Within less than a year after this event, Humáyún retired towards Kandahar, which was held by his brother Mirza Askári, in whose hands the infant Akbar was left, while his unlucky sire proceeded to Herat and Kazvin, whence he sent messengers to Ispahan to implore the friendly offices of Shah Tahmasp, king of Persia.

It is related of Sher Khan that early in life he imbibed the idea of driving the Mughals from India, and that Bábar, at whose table he one day ate his dinner with his dagger, for want of a knife, remarked, "This Afghan is not to be disconcerted with trifles. He may become a great man yet." And he did, too great for the house of Bábar.

Sher Khan, now called Sher Shah, had hardly expelled Humáyún, when he had to put down a revolt by his own lieutenant in Bengal, after which he proceeded to conquer Malwa, in the course of which he put to death the garrison of Raísúr, which had capitulated upon terms, and to invade Marwar in 1544. In that sterile tract of Rajputana he wasted so much time and money and so many men, that when he had reduced it to submission, he declared that for a handful of grain he had nearly lost the empire of India. He next took Chitor and besieged Kalinjar, in Bandelkand, where he was wounded by the blowing up of a magazine, and died the same night on hearing news of the capture of the fort, saying, "Thanks be to God." He was a prince of great talent for war and administration. From Bengal to the Indus, a distance of two thousand miles, he built caravanserais and wells at intervals of two or three miles, and mosques at longer intervals, and he planted avenues along the roads, and so ordered his police arrangements that it was said that in his day merchants and travellers put down upon the road their property and slept without apprehension. To one who remarked that his beard was growing white, he replied that he had been elevated to the throne late in life—a circumstance he regretted only because it had given him too short a time to devote to the welfare of his country and its inhabitants.

Sher Shah's second son, Selim Shah, succeeded him in 1545, supplanting the eldest son, after the usual intrigues and conspiracies, and reigned for nine tranquil years. It was in regard to the succession of this prince that the famous words were spoken, "Empire is no man's inheritance, but belongs to him who hath the longest sword." Like his father, he was a great builder of caravanserais.

His brother-in-law, Muhammad Shah Adili, reigned in his stead, one whom the Hindus called the blind or foolish. He used to discharge among the people, when he rode out, gold-headed arrows, worth from ten to twelve rupees. He soon disgusted his nobles by conferring their estates upon low-born favourites, "sellers of dogs." While he was quelling a revolt at Chanár, one of his family seized Delhi and Agra, which he kept, the king remaining in the territories to the east of Chanár. Under another relative the Punjab revolted, and one and the same prince, Sikandur Sur, soon possessed Delhi, Agra, and the Punjab. Meanwhile Ḥumáyún returned to India, and Hému reduced a revolt in Bengal and took Agra. Humáyún died just now, and was succeeded by Akbar, a youth of thirteen years, whose minister, Bairám, defeated Hému in a great battle at Pánípat on November 5, 1556, while Queen Mary was reigning in England, and endeavouring to extirpate the Protestant religion, which had been adopted twenty years before, while the great battle between traditional authority and free inquiry between the Church of Rome and her revolted children was beginning in France in the reign of Henry II.

Though Humáyún reigned but a few precarious months after his return to Delhi, his history during his long exile in Persia calls for brief notice. Shah Tahmasp, the second of the house of Safavi or Sophi kings, was a bigoted Shiyya. It is hard to understand why, because the Shiyya holds the three Caliphs who succeeded Muhammad to be usurpers, and Ali, his son-in-law, the fourth Caliph, his first rightful successor, therefore a deadly feud should have existed to this day between him and his brother Sunni, who holds that Abubakr, Omar, and Othman were lawfully elected successors of the Prophet by virtue of their selection by the congregation at Medina. But such is the fact. The breach arose out of the assassination of Ali and the subsequent civil war, and the death of Hussein, the son of Ali, upon the sandy plain of Kerbela.

The Shiyyas hold that the divine right resides in Ali and his descendants; that the chief duty of religion consists in devotion to the *Imam* or Pontiff. "The word *Imam*," says the Rev. Edward Sell, than whom there is no greater living authority on questions relating to the laws, religion, and languages of the Muhammadans, "means a leader or exemplar." The Lord said to Abraham, "I am about to make thee an '*Imam*' to mankind." The Shiyya believes it to be God's will that the *Imamat* should continue in the family of Ali; that the splendour of God, a ray of light from His own body, which was united with that of Muhammad, descends through the line of Ali to the true Imams. They assert the unity of God, whose chief Prophet is Muhammad, to whom succeeded Ali, and the twelve Imams from Ali to Abu'l Gasur, the Imam Madhi, who is still alive, though hidden in some secret place, whence he will reappear.

Mr. Sell has observed that the rationale of the Shiyya doctrine is the natural desire in the human heart for a mediator between God and man, the philosophic basis of the worship of Christ and of the adoration of the blessed Virgin to this day. At the Muharrum feast, the dynastic difference and the death of Ali and his sons are celebrated. The line of cleavage divides the Muhammadan world in two.

Shah Ismail, the father of the host of Humáyún, formally established the Shiyya doctrine in Persia, and the Ottoman Sultan, Selim I., when in 1516 he conquered Egypt, sought from Mutawakal, the last Caliph of the house of Abbas, the transfer of the Caliphate to himself. Hence the Sultan of Turkey's claim to the Caliphate, which is acknowledged by the Sunni division of the Muhammadans, though they are not, as Caliphs and Imams must rightly be, of the Prophet's own tribe of the Koreish. In India, where the Muhammadans are chiefly Sunnis, the prayer for the ruler is said for the Sultan; and the Sultans of Rum are no doubt as much Caliphs as Charlemagne and his successors were emperors of Rome.

Shah Tahmasp was naturally a bigoted Shiyya, and though he received Humáyún with the pomp and circumstance befitting a great monarch, not long after his arrival he sent him a supply of firewood, with an intimation that it should serve as his funeral-pyre if he did not conform to the religion of the country; and it appears that the Padshah did nominally conform, and even promised to introduce the Shiyya doctrines into India, as well as to cede Kandahar to the Persian Shah, who thereupon undertook to provide Humáyún with an army to help him to recover his kingdom. The latter prince, in 1545, marched to Bost, upon the Helmand, the frequent scene of strife between the Afghans, after more than three hundred years, and thence to Kandahar, and took the fort from his brother Mizra Askari, who was compelled to appear before him with a naked sword hung about his neck.

Kandahar was made over to the Persians, but Humáyún subsequently became repossessed of it, and also occupied Kábul, when he recovered his son Akbar, who had remained there during his father's absence in Persia. For the next two years Humáyún was engaged in fighting with his brother Kámrán, who was delivered into his hands by the Ghakkar spearmen and was blinded. No person could for a while be found willing to undertake the operation, and the sufferer, while undergoing it, called out, "My God! my sins have been amply punished in this world; have compassion upon me in the next." In 1555, when, on the death of Muhammad Shah, Sikandar Shah and Ibráhím were disputing for his dominions, Humáyún marched to India, took Lahore, and defeated Sikandar, seized Delhi and Agra, where he reigned over a part of his former kingdom for six months. He met his death by falling from a marble staircase at Delhi, in the forty-ninth year of his age and the twenty-sixth of his reign, of which he spent sixteen years in banishment.

CHAPTER V.

HINDU INDIA.

I. POLITICAL HISTORY FROM 1001 A.D.

THE whole of India became more or less subject to the great Akbar, who in 1556 succeeded his father Humáyún, and this will be a convenient opportunity for briefly noticing the growth of Hinduism up to the sixteenth century, the Hindu kingdoms of the south, the Muhammadan states of the Dekhan, and the internal state of India under the Muhammadan Empire up to the days of Akbar.

It has been seen already that, in addition to the aboriginal inhabitants of India, the population is made up of the races which entered the country in prehistoric times, presumably from Central Asia, who are commonly called Aryans, though their origin has been the subject of more dogmatism than discovery, and Scythians or Tartars, who had previously, to use the words of Sir William Hunter, "roamed over the plains of Central Asia with their cattle, and whose one talent was for war." About 500 B.C. the Buddhist religion widened the sphere of Brahmanism, which previously had occupied a position akin to that now occupied by Confucianism in China, of a state code of morals. Buddhism till 400 A.D. served to weld together in a more harmonious whole the centrifugal forces then at work in India. In the seventh century Brahmanism began to gain the upper hand, and in the ninth it had completely triumphed over its rival. In its present aspect it represents, to quote Hunter, the union of the Vedic faith of the early Brahmans with Buddhism and with the ruder rites of the aboriginal tribes of India. The Brahman pantheism is sufficiently comprehensive to include all within its tolerant fold. If the English dominion in India ceased, and the missionaries left with their compatriots, it is not unlikely that the Brahmans would adopt the few low-caste converts to Christianity. Christ they might represent, like Ráma, as an avatar or incarnation of one of the great gods, and some of the Christian missionaries would probably be canonised for their noble and self-sacrificing lives. It is only to Europeans that this toleration seems strange. In the neighbouring empire of China, one and the same man may be a Shintoist and a follower of Confucius, will certainly worship his own ancestors, and will perhaps be a bit of a Buddhist into the bargain. The Christians are few, for they are but 0·73 per cent. of the population of India, and of the fractional total Christian population nearly three-quarters (74½ per cent.) are found in Madras, Travancore, Haidarábád, Mysore, and Cochin.

To this day the gods of the villagers are for the most part vermilion-streaked stones or stems of trees and lumps of clay. Of the great divines, one of the greatest was Sankara Achárya, who in the ninth century laboured to popularise his religion and to determine the adoration of the millions towards Siva in his several manifestations of the Destroyer and Reproducer, and of his wife Devi, Durga, or Káli. These in their various aspects sufficed as manifestations of the deity to the learned and the unlettered, to the Brahman and the aboriginal inhabitant. In the eleventh century the Vishnu Purána crystallised the doctrines of the worship of Vishnu, the Preserver, who in his incarnations of Ráma and Krishna is worshipped throughout India. The great Vishnavite doctor was Rámánuja, who flourished in the middle of the twelfth century and proclaimed the unity of God, to whom succeeded Rámanand in the fourteenth and Chaitánya in the sixteenth century, a liberal apostle, who held that all castes by faith became equally pure, that by incessant devotion the soul should be freed from the restraints of the vile body. His sect first acknowledged the equal position of women in religion and in domestic life. Subsequently Vallabha Swami developed the epicurean and pleasure-loving aspects of Vaishnavism, of which, too, outward and visible signs are to be found in the pictorial and carved presentments of religious subjects found in temples and on temple cars. In spite of the efforts of missionaries throughout India, and especially in the South, there is no proof that Hinduism is in any way losing its hold over the people. The towers of the great pagodas of Southern India proudly rear their heads above the humble spires of the little Christian churches, and that the day of equality or of superiority is as far off as ever may be inferred even more from the indifferent tolerance of the Hindus than from the small number of recruits from the lowest castes who have hitherto undertaken to carry the Cross in India.

To the south of the Vindhya range, the convenient and traditional boundary between Hindustan and the Dekhan, flourished prior to the foundation of the Mughal empire the three Hindu kingdoms of Chera, Chola, and Pandya, the capitals of which were at their most important epochs situated in Mysore, at Tanjore, and at Madura respectively. The history of these ancient kingdoms belongs to another volume of this series; it will suffice here to say that long lines of kings are enumerated by native historians, and that a native Hindu dynasty survived in the extreme south till the eighteenth century. With the Hindu kingdom of Vijáyanagar, however, Muhammadan history is more intimately connected. It lasted from 1118 till 1565, and during this period successfully competed with the Muhammadan kingdoms of the Dekhan for the supremacy of Southern India. The ramparts of the capital can still be traced among the solitary and stony hills near Humpi,[1] on the right bank of the Tungabadra, in the Bellary district of the Madras Presidency, and some of its many palaces and temples are still in fair repair.

It has already been stated that in the reign of Muhammad Tughlak (1324–1351), the contemporary of Edward III. and Richard II. of England, and of Philip de Valois of France, the empire of Delhi extended from the Himálayas and the Indus on the north-west and north-east to the sea on the east and west, with the exception of the kingdom of Orissa, which stretched from the Ganges to the Godáveri, and such portions of Rajputana as were still independent. The South, too, for the most part acknowledged the supremacy of Delhi. During Muhammad Tughlak's reign Telingána and Karnata recovered their independence at Warangal and Vijáyanagar respectively, and brought the extreme south of the Peninsula into dependence more or less complete upon their dynasties. After the death of Muhammad Tughlak, Gujarat, Malwa, and Júánpur, or the country on the Ganges from Bengal to Oudh, became independent; and in 1398, upon the invasion of Tamerlane, all the provinces of the empire threw off their allegiance.

The greatest of the independent Muhammadan kingdoms which then came into existence was that of the

[1] See *Tours in India*, by J. D. Rees, p. 15 *seq.*

Báhmani kings, so called from the fact that Zafar Khan, its founder, had once been the slave of a Brahman, who treated him well and foretold the future greatness of his house. The Báhmani dynasty had its capital at Warangal and Bidar in Haidarabad, to which modern state it more or less accurately corresponds. It subjugated the kingdom of Warangal and conquered the country between the Krishna and the Tungabadra, and its conquests extended to Masulipatam on the east, and Goa on the west coast. The army of the kings of this house were composed of Persian Shiyyas, and Central Asian Turks and Tartars, and of native-born Mussalmans of Southern India; and their rivalries resulted finally in the break up of the kingdom, and between 1489 and 1688 there flourished no less than five Muhammadan states in the Dekhan, which were formed out of its fragments. These were the Adil Sháhi kingdom of Bijapur, the Kutab Sháhi kingdom of Golkonda, the Nizam Sháhi dynasty of Ahmadnagar, the Imád Sháhi dynasty of Elichpur, and the Baríd Sháhi dynasty of Bidar.

The kings of Bijapur ruled from 1489–1688, when the kingdom was annexed by Aurangzeb. Its founder, Yusuf Adil Shah, is reputed to have been a son of Amurath II., and brother of Muhammad II., the Ottoman conqueror of Constantinople, who fled to Persia when the brothers of the king were put to death, became a Mamluk slave at the court of the Bahmani king, and finally a successful and intrepid general. He was a bigoted Shiyya, and religious difficulties and differences harassed the state during his reign and those of his successors. During the reign of the sixth king of this house, who ascended the throne in 1579, his neighbours in the Western Gháts, the Maráthás, rose to notice, and were freely employed in his service against the Hindu kings of Vijáyanagar. In 1570 an unsuccessful effort was made by the king of the day to expel the Portuguese from Goa, but in 1565 he had, in concert with the four other Muhammadan kings of the Dekhan, crushed the king of Vijáyanagar at the great battle of Talikót, on the Krishna, in 1565, after which the southern portions of the dominions of that house became independent under native princes, zemindars, and poligars. The brother of the deceased Rája moved to Chandragiri, a little to the north-west of Madras, where a picturesque old palace is still pointed out as his dwelling-place, and there his descendants granted in 1640 to the English the land upon which Fort St. George now stands. The Mahárájas of Mysore are descended from the local representative of the kings of Vijáyanagar, close to the ruins of which, across the river, dwells a descendant in the female line of the royal house, the impoverished Zemindar of Anagundi. The dynasty of Ahmadnagar was founded in 1490 by the son of a Brahman village-accountant of Bijapur, who had been a slave of the Báhmani king, and became a devout Mussalman, and was subverted by Sháh Jahán in 1636. An enormous cannon, taken from the Nizám Sháh by the king of Bijapur, may now be seen upon the walls of the latter city. The ruins of Bijapur attest the greatness of that kingdom; they are of wide extent, and some of them still of great beauty. The exquisite proportions, profuse yet graceful ornament, and lace-like carvings of the mausoleum of Ibrahim Adil Sháh excite the admiration of visitors familiar with the Taj and other masterpieces of Saracenic architecture, while Sultan Mahmúd reposes beneath the largest dome in the world, which crowns a suitably imposing mass of plain masonry. Architects have fully described this wondrous work, astonished at a covered area of upwards of 18,000 square feet, uninterrupted by supports. They compare it with the Pantheon, the next largest space covered by a single dome, and with St. Paul's, with which it is contemporary. The buildings are of a widely different character, and all technicalities apart, the Bijapur dome may be described as resembling an inverted teacup, while that of the Pantheon favours the form of an inverted saucer.

The historian Ferishta, who himself resided in Bijapur in 1589, and completed his History, after a long residence in that capital, in 1609, gives some interesting details of life in a Muhammadan capital in Southern India in his time. He describes a virtuous prince as one who, when he rides through the streets of a city, looks neither right nor left, lest his eyes should fall upon another's wife; and referring to the practice of duelling, which he says had become very prevalent, he thus narrates an encounter of which he was an eye-witness:—Syud Murtuza and Syud Hussein, two brothers whose beards were grey, and who were in high estimation at court, had a trifling dispute with three Dekhanis, who were also brothers who frequented the court, and were also respectable and grey-headed men. First the son of Syud Murtuza, a youth of twenty, engaged one of the Dekhanis, but was immediately killed. The father and uncle engaged the other two Dekhanis, and they also were killed; and before their bodies could be removed and buried, the three opponents died of the wounds they had received, so that in a few minutes six respectable persons, who had no real animosity towards each other, were lost to their relations and to society. For a vivid picture drawn from historical sources of life at the courts of Bijapur and Ahmadnagar, the reader may safely turn to the pages of Colonel Meadows Taylor's "Noble Queen."

The founder of the Kutab Sháhi dynasty of Golkonda was a Turkman, from the beautiful city of Hamadan, the

Ecbatana of the Medes, which still supplies the hardiest soldiers of the Shah of Persia, and he entered the service of the Bahmani king, of whom he became independent in 1512, and ruled over the old Telingána kingdom of Warangal, and parts of the Vijáyanagar territory, to which subsequently were added the present northern districts of the Madras Presidency, the Kistna, Godáveri, Vizagapatam, and Ganjam districts, as well as those of Cuddapah and Nellore. The fourth king of this house built Haidarabád, which he called Bhagnagar, and moved his capital thence from Golkonda. The kingdom was annexed by Aurangzeb in 1688.

The Muhammadan kings of Bidar and Berar were of comparatively small importance; but the kingdoms of Gujarat and Malwa, which became independent after the invasion of Tamerlane, are worthy of attention in the briefest history. The former lasted from 1391 till 1573, when it was conquered by Akbar, after it had annexed Malwa in 1531. Lower Bengal had been independent since 1340, and though temporarily annexed by Humáyún, as already related, it was not finally included in the empire of Delhi till 1576 by Akbar.

The kingdom of Gujarat was founded in 1391 by the son of a Rajput convert during the reign at Delhi of Firuz Tughlak. The greatest of its kings were Ahmad Shah and Mahmúd, who reigned from 1459 to 1511. It is useless to follow these minor dynasties through weary and unremembered wars; but Mahmúd of Gujarat was famous upon the sea as well as the land, and kept the pirates of the western coast in subjection. He also helped the Mamluk Sultan of Egypt in making war against the Portuguese in India, and the combined fleets were routed in 1508 in an action off Diu, on the Kathiawar peninsula, which still belongs to his most faithful Majesty of Portugal. For many years afterwards the Mamluks sent fleets to open the navigation of the Red Sea and the Persian Gulf. Mahmúd's successor in 1511 received an embassy from Sháh Ismaíl of Persia, who was then zealously engaged in obtaining converts to the Shiyya faith. The war of Bahádur Sháh in 1433 with Humáyún has already been noticed, but not the fact of that king having allowed the Portuguese to build a factory at Diu in return for their aid, and a quarrel between the king and the Portuguese viceroy resulted in an affray in which Bahádur Sháh lost his life. The country was a prey to rebellion and anarchy from 1538 till the date of its conquest by Akbar.

Besides the Hindu and Muhammadan kingdoms above mentioned, there remain, however, the Rajput states, which had never been conquered, whose strong forts, hilly country, sandy deserts, and brave spirits have preserved their independence.

At the accession of Akbar the Ránas of Chitor were independent, though they had been defeated by Bahádur Sháh of Gujarat, and had acknowledged the supremacy of Sher Sháh of Delhi, and so were the Rájas of Marwar, of Jhodpur, of Jaisalmir. The Rájas of Jaipur, who then resided at Amber, where their romantic castle still remains, had been feudatories of Ajmir, which had been subdued by the Muhammadans. The small states on the east of Rajputana, which were more open to attacks and nearer to Delhi and Agra, such as Mewat and Gwalior, were already subject to the Muhammadans, while the small Hindu states in and along the Terai at the foot of the Himálayas, from Kashmir to the Bay of Bengal, were ruled by their own indigenous chiefs.

II. Internal Condition of India in the Sixteenth Century.

From the works of the historian Elphinstone, and from the various publications of the Hakluyt Society, some idea may be obtained of the internal state of India in the beginning of the sixteenth century and in the fifteenth century, prior to the Portuguese discovery of the Cape of Good Hope, and from the authorities to whom reference has been made in Chapter I. some information has been gathered as to the trade which was carried on between Rome and India by way of the Red Sea, which began to decline after the partition of the former empire, or to be supplanted by trade with Constantinople by caravan through Persia. The intercourse between India and the Byzantine Empire was, however, interrupted by the Arab conquest, and their trade with the west by their hostilities with the Christians in Europe. In the tenth century the republics of Amalfi and Venice reopened intercourse with India by way of Egypt; and in the eleventh century the irruptions of the Turks into Syria and Palestine led to commercial intercommunications between east and west to an extent previously unknown, which was chiefly carried on by the republics of Genoa and Venice. Upon the expulsion of the Genoese from Constantinople in 1453 the Venetians monopolised the trade between the East and the ports of the Mamluk Sultans of Egypt in that country and in Syria till the close of the fifteenth century, when the discovery of America and the rounding of the Cape threw the commerce of India into the hands of the Portuguese. Nicolo de Conti, whose travels ended in 1444, dilates upon the greatness of Vijáyanagar, refers to the ships upon the Ganges made of bamboo, to the use of palm leaves for writing, which continues to this day. Abd-er-Razzáh, who was ambassador in 1442 from Sháh Rukh of Persia to the king of Vijáyanagar, gives an account of the splendour of that city; and the Russian traveller Nikitin in 1470 dwells upon the magnificence of the Muhammadan court of Bidar, remarking that the people none the less were wretched and miserable. Perhaps, however, the contrast was only that natural between capital and country. The Muhammadan court at Haidarabád in the present day is in striking contrast with the Hindu villages of that state, but it can hardly be alleged that the people are wretched and miserable. The Portuguese traveller, Barbosa, in the beginning of the sixteenth century, gives an account of the kingdom of Gujarat, from which we may infer that its inhabitants were generally prosperous and well-dressed, and possessed of funds for amusement and even luxury. He says the country was so rich and well supplied as to attract Turks, Mamluks, Arabs, Persians, Khorassans, and Turkmans, and that the Moors or Muhammadans of Kambay lived well and spent much money. He refers to the mediæval legend of the father of the king of the day, whose daily food was asp and basilisk and toad, who in making himself poison-proof had become so impregnated with poison that if a fly settled on his hand it swelled and died, and that wives with whom he but once slept died of his poisonous proximity. Barbosa describes the fertility of the country, the roofed and tiled houses of the towns, and their orchards and gardens, the active trade of Diu, the cloth and silk manufactures of Kambay, the skill of its artisans in working in ivory, silver, and wood, the trade of the western coast in cocoa and areca nuts, spices, and drugs. This writer gives an excellent account also of the Malabar coast and the kingdom of Vijáyanagar.

From contemporary records referred to now and

again in these pages, and chiefly from the chronicles of Ferishta, it appears that the Muhammadan kings were easy of access, and as a rule themselves disposed of much business, usually more or less in conformity with the laws of Islam, subject to which their authority was absolute. Such authority was, however, freely delegated to the governors of provinces, who again exercised practically absolute authority, except over such chiefs as were more or less independent. The army was chiefly composed of chiefs who supplied fighting men fully equipped, or of individual soldiers who served for hire, and governors of provinces had to supply troops to the imperial army. The law was administered by Kázis, or doctors learned in the Koran, and by the officers of government, civil questions and offences not relating to affairs of state or the public peace being generally adjudicated upon by the former officers. To the officers of Government Elphinstone assigns disputes between Hindus and revenue differences, offences against the state and the public peace. There was no established Church, in the sense in which the words are used in England. Mosques were founded and priests supported by private endowments, and the British Government has charged itself with the duty of seeing that such funds are devoted to the purposes for which they were originally given. Judges, lawyers, and ministers were chosen from the class of Moulvis or Mollahs, who had graduated in an informal way in law and divinity, and must on no account be confounded with the fakirs, who professed poverty and abstinence, whereby they pretended to have acquired peculiar sanctity and even supernatural powers, their claims to which by degrees came to be more or less admitted by orthodox Muhammadans, though not sanctioned by the Koran.

The Hindus were on the whole treated with tolerant leniency, but had to pay a poll-tax; they were largely employed in the administration, and sometimes as military commanders. Bábar in his memoirs says that on his arrival "the officers of revenue, merchants, and workpeople were all Hindus." That the Muhammadan conquerors, who arrived in India after the first flush of enthusiasm had subsided, were on the whole tolerant and moderate in proselytism, is proved by the fact that the number of conversions was but small.

Coined silver and gold were used throughout the Mussulman domination. Sher Sháh was the first to use the rupee, which was fixed by Akbar at a weight not far different to that of the present coin. By the time of Akbar, the Indian Muhammadans had adopted their muslin robes and slippers, and their manners and customs had undergone a corresponding change since their descent from the uplands of Central Asia. This approximation to the customs of the country of their adoption was encouraged for political reasons by Akbar.

As the connection with Persia became slighter, and fell off after the adoption by that country of the Shiyya heresy, literature decayed, and a language, the roots of which were Sanscrit, came to be spoken by the invaders, which in the beginning of the fifteenth century began to approximate to Hindustani.

CHAPTER VI.

THE MUGHALS—(*Continued*).

I. AKBAR (1556–1605).

WHEN Akbar ascended the throne in 1556, he was but thirteen years old, and Bairám Khán, a Turkman noble, the confidential minister of the father, continued to occupy the same position under the son, whom he confirmed on the throne of Delhi by defeating Sikandar Sur, and Hému, whose head he cut off with his own hand. Continued success and prosperity had the effect of bringing out into stronger relief the harsh and tyrannical character of Bairám, and the Padshah chafed under the restraints imposed upon him by the real ruler of the state, until he put to death more than one highly placed officer of state, without so much as formally taking his master's orders. Then Akbar determined to free himself, and, under the familiar pretext of the illness of his mother, he left the minister's protection while both were engaged upon a hunting expedition, and hastening to Delhi, announced that he had assumed the conduct of affairs. The regent, after in vain attempting to recover his position, rebelled, but being defeated, delivered himself up to Akbar, who forgave him and dismissed him upon a pilgrimage to Mecca, upon which he was about to start when he was assassinated by an Afghan whose father he had slain in battle. The Padshah was now, in 1560, but eighteen years of age; he was handsome in person, pleasant in manner, of great personal strength and of undaunted courage. The house of Tamerlane had no base upon which to draw, as had the kings of Ghor and Ghazní, and the recent expulsion of Humáyún made his son careful to broad base his empire upon the will of the peoples of India, and to the realisation of this ideal he steadily devoted himself through a long and glorious reign. But at the outset he had to acquire the provinces which had shaken off the yoke of Delhi. He soon subdued Ajmír, Gwalior, Lucknow, and the eastern country as far as the confines of Bengal, and his general Khán Zeman defeated the son of the last king of the Sur dynasty.

The invasions of an earlier date than that of Tamerlane had left behind in India a population of Turks and Afghans under their own chiefs, and one of these, Baz Bahádur, had to be expelled by force from Malwa. Adham Khán defeated him, and his Hindu mistress, celebrated for her beauty, fell into the victor's hands. By the custom of the time, he succeeded to her favours, and when she had resisted in vain, she appointed an hour for their meeting, and, dressed in her most magnificent gown, reclining on pillows in a silken pavilion, she awaited his arrival with a veil over her face. On the removal of the veil it was found she was dead, and had taken poison rather than prove unfaithful to her lord and master. But Adham Khan was no more loyal to his king than generous to the unfortunate, and he stabbed Akbar's vizier, who was saying his prayers in an upper room next the king's, whence he was hurled, as a punishment, to the paven floor far below. The governor of Malwa, an Uzbek by race, next rebelled, and other Uzbeks joined him. Akbar triumphed, however, against all combinations, including one made in the Punjab by his brother Hákim, and another by Khán Zeman in Oude, in the course of suppressing which he swam the Ganges in the rains with 2000 men, and attacked the unsuspecting enemy on the other side, killed Khán Zeman, and put the enemy to flight. Prince Hákim had been driven out of Kábul, to the government of which he had succeeded on the death of Humáyún, when he seized Lahore, but he returned to that country after he had in 1566 been expelled from India by Akbar.

In the *Akbarnáma* is related an account of the way in which the Padshah settled a religious disturbance. He came one day upon two bodies of Hindus prepared to fight for the possession of a sacred bathing-place, and after in vain endeavouring to compose their strife, he let them fight it out and saw fair play. This simple method of settling such matters may be compared with the infinite pains taken in the present day to prevent disturbances between rival sectaries, which in fact now seldom occur.

In 1567 Akbar turned his attention to the Rajputs, and first attacked the Raja of Chitor, whose fortress was bravely defended by his general, Jai Mal. From the narrative of Ferishta it appears that Akbar approached gradually behind successive rows of trenches in order to get sufficiently near to sink mines, which, owing to miscalculations, proved as dangerous to the assailants as to the besieged. Akbar, however, shot Jai Mal with his own hand as he superintended the defence by torchlight upon the battlements, whereupon the women were burnt with the brave chieftain's body and the Rajputs rushed forth to death. Chitor was taken, but the Rana's son subsequently recovered part of his heritage and founded Udaipur, where his posterity still reign, as feudatory princes under the British imperial protection. The Rája of Jaipur was reduced, and his daughter married to the Padshah, as was a princess of Marwa, and the grand-daughter of the submissive Rája of Jodhpur was given to the heir-apparent, Prince Salim, afterwards Jahángír. By such connections Akbar hoped, and not without reason, to conciliate the high-born and high-spirited Rajputs, and to reconcile them to the Muhammadan supremacy.

In 1572 he was invited to put an end to the internal dissensions of the Muhammadan kingdom of Gujarat, to which a brief reference has already been made, the youthful and nominal king of which voluntarily resigned his crown to the Padshah in order to escape from the oppression of the Mirzas, princes of the house of Tamerlane, who had revolted against the Emperor, and had been compelled to fly to Gujarat for safety. After an adventurous campaign, Gujarat was reannexed to the crown of Delhi, and in 1576 Akbar recovered Bengal from the Afghan prince of the family of Sher Sháh, which had held it since 1539, whose name was Dáúd Khán. With Bengal the province of Bihar was also acquired. But the troops mutinied, and Akbar's chiefs, who hoped to reap the fruits of the victory, revolted against the payment of revenue to the imperial exchequer, while the Afghan adherents of the dispossessed dynasty rebelled against their new masters and seized the Muhammadan province of Orissa, a small portion of the country of that name. Here they rendered themselves odious to the inhabitants by confiscating the revenues of the great temple of Gaganatha or Juggernaut, and the Emperor taking advantage of their impolitic conduct, was enabled thereby to complete the conquest of Bengal.

In 1586 Akbar first entertained the project of annexing Kashmir, which, in the fourteenth century, had been taken by an enterprising Muhammadan chief from its native Hindu princes. Domestic dissension soon provided the necessary pretext, and after experiencing such difficulties as are inherent in the conquest of a mountainous country, Kashmir was reduced to submission, and formed from that time forward the summer retreat of the great Mughals and of their courtiers, who had not yet forgotten, in the burning plains of Hindustan, the cool and bracing uplands whence they came, and whence they brought the stock of strength and energy which enabled them to conquer India.

The Afghans were now to feel the weight of the Emperor's arm, and the greatest of the great Mughals was to find these hardy mountaineers as difficult to deal with as the English in turn have found them. Rája Bir Bal, the favourite of the Padshah, was drawn into an ambuscade in the hills of Swat and slain; stones were rolled down upon his soldiers; the Afghans rushed down in the midst of the confusion, and the imperial troops were routed and retreated with considerable loss to Attok. Though the courtly historian of the reign says that the Afgháns were subsequently reduced to complete submission, it is more probable that they continued to enjoy a rude and precarious independence, as did the Roushenías, or followers of Báyazíd, a pretended prophet, whose principles included that of plundering all those of a different religion—a doctrine most grateful to the turbulent spirit of the Afghans. The first war of a ruler of united Hindustan with the Afghans was contemporaneous with the war between Philip of Spain and Elizabeth, and the destruction of the Invincible Armada. In 1591 Sindh was annexed, and its ruler made one of the chief nobles of the Mughal court. The conflict with the ruler of this country is memorable from the fact that Portuguese soldiers and native soldiers in European uniform fought in his service.

In 1594 Akbar recovered Kandahár from the lieutenant of Sháh Abbas of Persia, with whom, however, he maintained friendly relations, and by this time he had extended the Mughal empire from Afghanistan across the whole of India north of the Vindhya mountains, including Sindh upon the west, and Orissa to the east. He now moved the seat of government to the more central position of Agra, and founded Fatehpur Síkri, which he intended to be the imperial capital.

In the Dekhan, however, ominous field as it had proved before, and will again, for the Mughal arms, he was less successful. Internal dissensions among the members of the Nizam Sháhi family of Ahmadnagar provided the welcome pretext, but the capital was in the hands of the famous Queen Chand Bibi, who held it for her nephew, and she appealed to the king of Bijapur, her kinsman, who helped her with an army, while internal dissensions were for the while composed in the presence of a common foe. The queen superintended the construction of the counter-mines, and when a breach was made by the Mughals, and her troops were about to retreat from the walls, she herself, sword in hand, clad in armour, but wearing a veil, by her heroic conduct recalled them to a sense of duty, and drove back the enemy. A peace was concluded in 1566, and Akbar rested for a few months, when war again broke out with Ahmadnagar, with which kingdom the kings of Golkonda and Bijapur had joined to oppose the Mughal conquest of the Dekhan. Abul Fazl, a man of the sword as well as the pen, the writer of the *Akbarnáma*, was in command, but he represented to the Padshah that his presence was necessary; and Akbar, who never spared himself, at once came southwards and proceeded to besiege Ahmadnagar; and the queen, Chand Bibi, being hard set by domestic faction and treason, was negotiating with the enemy for an honourable evacuation of the city, when the "short-sighted and ungrateful Dekhanis" rushed into her private apartment and put her to death, within a few days of which occurrence the Mughals took

Ahmadnagar, though the dynasty of Ahmad Sháh continued to reign there, with diminished glory and resources, till Sháh Jahán finally put an end to it in 1637. Of Chand Bibi many tales are told in the Dekhan to this day. A native historian relates that she fired copper, silver, and gold coins at the Mughals when iron was exhausted, and was firing away the crown jewels when death quieted her valorous soul.

After annexing the country of Khándesh, which lay between Gujarat and Berar, and marrying one of his sons to a daughter of the king of Bijapur, Akbar returned to Agra in 1601, the year in which the first East India Company was formed, and in which the first English ships reached India. He returned none too soon, for his son Salim, afterwards Jahángír, who used to drink five quarts of wine a day, and eat opium to excess, had seized Oudh and Bihar and the royal treasure, and assumed the style of king.

The Padshah dissembled or overcame his resentment, and confirmed his rebellious son in the government of Bengal and Orissa, for which he was rewarded by the treacherous murder, at the order of Salim, of his faithful friend and minister, Abul Fazl. Salim defends this act and his rebellion in his memoirs by declaring that the minister had seduced his father from the true faith, from which indeed Akbar had somewhat widely departed. The behaviour of his heir embittered the last years of Akbar's life and glorious reign. Nor did his other sons prove a comfort to him. Dánial died of drink, and Murád was cut off before his father. In the autumn of 1605 the great Padshah sickened, and on October 13, 1605, it was obvious that the end was near. His rebellious heir was admitted to the dying man's chamber, together with the chief nobles of the court, and to them and their protection he commended him, and ordered him to be girt with the royal scimitar. He then with kindly and affectionate solicitude, which characterised him throughout life, urged upon his successor the care of the ladies of his family, and repeating the orthodox confession of faith, quietly left that world in which he had played so great a part. His cheerful disposition, amiable manners, and pleasing person endeared him to his courtiers and to his people, and, in spite of his great talents for war and administration, he delighted in, and found time for, study and sport. Though brave and adventurous, he was no knight-errant, nor did he wantonly make war on any king or country after he recovered all the countries that ever had, in the widest sense of the word, been subject to, or held by Delhi.

The publication, just after the poet's death, of Tennyson's "Akbar's Dream," has directed public attention to the religion of this Padshah, who inclined to tolerate Hinduism, and even to invent a new religion, which might comprehend all classes of his subjects. He dreamt of an eclecticism embracing all that was best in Islám, Hinduism, Christianity, Buddhism, and Judaism. Probably he was to a great extent sincere, probably, like other kings of his day, notably Henry IV. of France, who thought Paris worth a mass, his religion sat lightly upon him, and was subservient in some measure to his political interests. In order to a thorough examination of religious matters, the sacred books of the Hindus were translated, and a Christian priest was brought from Goa, and Akbar's most intimate friends engaged in constant argument with their master, who delighted in religious symposia, at which the adherents to different creeds were represented. The priests at one time entertained lively hopes that the Emperor would profess Christianity; but in fact Akbar was a deist, who saw "behind all creeds the godhead which is one," but, for the weakness of human nature, tolerated the outward and visible signs of various beliefs, especially that of the Zoroastrian, who made the glorious lamp of heaven, the sun, the visible object of his adoration. While he discarded ritual, he approved of abstinence and meditation; and while he claimed to be the Caliph of his own religion, he never pretended to the position of a prophet. Under his sway the bonds of Islam were greatly relaxed, and the use of wine was allowed, and the wearing of beards discouraged.

To the Hindus he permitted the liberty which he preached, but he allowed Hindu widows to marry a second time, discouraged Satí, and forbade marriage before the age of puberty. He thus anticipated the chief measures of reform adopted long after his day by "the alien race from out the sunset," under whose rule were neither

> "Seen nor heard
> Fires of Satí, nor wail of baby wife
> Or Indian widow."

Akbar's prohibition of infant marriage was a plank in the platform of the Age of Consent party two years ago, but the Mughals were not upon the whole so successful in their treatment of the Hindus as to make the precedent a happy one upon which to rely. He employed Hindus equally with Muhammadans in the administration, and abolished the capitation tax, the pilgrim impost, and the custom of making slaves of prisoners of war.

The Padshah's innovations in the field of religion, and perhaps not less his encouragement of Hindus and impartial attitude towards conquerors and conquered, provoked discontent among the orthodox Muslims and the Mollahs, fertile source in all times of political intrigue; but by firmness and clemency he overcame all such opposition, though eclecticism, then as now, proved unsuitable to the masses, made no progress during his life, and was speedily abandoned upon his death.

The revenue system of Akbar was merely a development of that which existed before his time, and was due to Sher Sháh, who was, as has already been remarked, an able administrator, and one who regretted that his life was not long enough to allow of his doing sufficient good to his people. Akbar caused to be measured, according to one uniform measurement, all the cultivable lands in the empire, which was divided into three classes according to its fertility, the demand of the state being fixed at one-third of the produce. Remissions, however, were granted when lands were actually uncultivated, and when they suffered from too much or too little water, in case the crops raised were such as required irrigation. The divisions of the soil into classes, and the methods of calculation of assessment, were not unlike those now followed by the Settlement Department of the Government of India. The tax of one-third of the produce was commuted into money payment on an average of the prices obtaining for the previous nineteen years, but it was considerately provided that any cultivator might claim to pay in kind if he considered the commutation rate too high.

The settlements made existed for ten years, as against the thirty years of the present British assessment. The measurements and classifications were recorded in the village accounts just as they are now. Among the instructions given to the collectors of the revenue is one which the Government of India equally impresses upon its officers, viz., that they should deal directly with the cultivators, and not trust too much to the village officers. Akbar's revenue minister was the celebrated Rája Todar Mal, and Abul Fazl, the finance minister who has already appeared in these pages in the character of a general, compiled the statistical account of the empire known as the *Aín-í-Akbarí*, from which the above particulars have been taken. Sir William Hunter has ascertained that the revenue derived from Northern India by the great Mughal exceeded that levied by the British, which is, of course, derived from many different sources, so that the land-tax is infinitely lighter in the present day; probably not more than one-third of what it was.

From fifteen provinces, including Kábul, the revenue derived was fourteen millions per annum. In addition to land-tax, the provinces had to support the local levies, and Hunter estimates the total revenue of Akbar at forty-two millions, about half of the amount now exacted from perhaps twice the area, in return for the manifold services of civilization now rendered by the state.

The viceroys of provinces had complete civil and military authority, and soldiers were paid as much as possible in money, and not by grants of land. Under a chief-justice at the capital were law-officers in the chief towns, in which also were superintendents of police called Kotwals. In the country districts there were no police, but the chief landowners were probably held more or less responsible for protection of life and property. An hereditary village police existed, but was frequently drawn from the robber classes. This system worked better than would be imagined, and till quite lately the village watchmen of the most southern part of India were of this character. Now that the British Government has changed all this, private owners in parts of the country inhabited by hereditary robbers still sometimes find it advisable to set one thief, who is generally true to his trust, to catch another.

Elaborate arrangements were made for the transport of troops, and fixed rates of payment laid down for provisions and carriage requisitioned by soldiers upon the march. Each troop or regiment was under the command of its chief, whose rank corresponded with the numbers he could bring into the field, and the troopers were generally men of the yeoman class, who supplied their own horses and weapons. The celebrated regiments of the Central India Horse, and many of the smart and efficient Bengal cavalry corps, are composed of this class of men, who, *cæteris paribus*, occupy much the same position in life as those who compose the British yeomanry cavalry. Matchlockmen, or infantry of the line, were paid 6 rupees per month, and archers 2½ rupees. When Abul Fazl says that the local militia amounted to 4,400,000 men, he probably gives a rough estimate of all the men capable of bearing arms, and theoretically bound to bear them, in the Padshah's service. No reliable estimate is available of the strength of Akbar's army, though in later times Bernier computed the cavalry of Aurangzeb at 200,000 sabres; and in drawing from this fact any deductions as to the probable strength of the infantry, it must not be forgotten that the relative proportion of cavalry to infantry is far greater in Asiatic than in European armies.

In the red stone fort of Agra, a splendid pile with curtains, towers, domes, and battlements, surrounded by a deep moat, may be seen to-day a specimen of the fortifications constructed by the great emperor, and in the ruins of Fatehpur Sikri examples of the mosques and palaces in which he prayed and lived.

The *Aín-i-Akbari* gives a full account not only of the civil and military administration, but of the stable, mint, garden, battery, and kennel. Ferishta says Akbar kept 5000 elephants and 12,000 horses, and 900 hunting leopards, from which the extent of his establishment in other departments may be imagined. Sir Thomas Roe has described the tent equipage of the great Mughal, its extent and magnificence, its square of 1530 yards in the centre of a city of tents, all of which may be seen, perhaps in somewhat lesser proportions, in the camps of the Viceroys of India of to-day, when they halt on the confines of the empire to receive, for instance, a visit from the Amir of Afghanistan. On festivals and holidays the Emperor was weighed against gold, and the amount scaled divided in largesse among the spectators, a custom which survives to this day with the Mahárájas of Travancore, Hindus of the Hindus, in the extreme south of the Peninsula. Amidst this splendour the Emperor charmed by the simplicity of his demeanour, a king "loved and feared of his own, and terrible only to his enemies."

II. Jahangir (1605–1627).

Prince Salim, when he succeeded his father in 1605, assumed the name of Jahángír, or World-Taker. He was the contemporary of James I. of England and Louis XIII. of France, and the earlier measures of his reign gave greater promise than might have been expected from his conduct during his father's lifetime. He retained his father's ministers and servants, though he abolished most of the religious ordinances of Akbar, and he adopted efficacious if whimsical measures for affording access to all petitioners at all times and seasons. The heir-apparent, Prince Khusru, following his father's example, rebelled, seized Lahore, gave battle to the Emperor, and was defeated. Jahángír impaled hundreds of his followers, and with refined cruelty caused Khusru to be led past them, in sorry imitation of the pomp and circumstance of an Indian durbar or reception.

In 1610 the affairs of Ahmadnagar imperatively demanded the attention of the Mughals, who had several times been defeated by the celebrated Málik Ambár, an Abyssinian, the minister of the king, Murtíza Nizam Sháh II. The justice and wisdom of Málik Ambár's administration have become proverbial in the Dekhan, and he was the founder of the city which, since the time of Aurangzeb, has been known as Aurangabad, and he introduced a revenue system similar to that of Raja Todar Mal into the Dekhan. At this time Jahángír married his empress, Núr Jahán, the Light of the World, a Persian by descent, born at Kandahar in such poor circumstances that she was exposed by the roadside, and brought up from compassion by a merchant, who engaged her own mother to nurse her. Through the kind offices of their patron, the family was advanced to a position more worthy of its original station, and Núr Jahán became the object of the attentions of Jahángír during the life of Akbar, who considering such an alliance inexpedient, married her to a Persian gentleman, and gave him an appointment out of the way in Bengal. But Jahángír did not forget his first love, and by his command his Viceroy of Bengal made such proposals to the husband as incited him to violence; whereupon he was slain by the viceroy's guard and his wife sent to Delhi, where the Emperor offered her marriage. From interested or sincere motives, however, she long declined to entertain the idea of marriage with one whom she naturally considered indirectly responsible for her husband's death. Her scruples were in the end overcome, and she became queen with such powers and privileges as no king probably, except Justinian alone, ever granted to his consort. She was consulted upon all affairs of state, her father was made vizier, and her name was engraved upon the coinage with that of the Emperor. She did not neglect the graces and accomplishments whence her power was derived, but spent much time and pains in the grateful care of her beauty, in providing fitting surroundings for such rare charms, and even in inventing and perfecting perfumes which might enhance their influence over the enslaved and besotted faculties of her drunken and imperial lord, who has been immortalised and idealised in the pages of "Lalla Rookh."

The calm of Jahángír's honeymoon, which the virtue or policy of the Empress had not allowed him to anticipate, was rudely broken by the ill success of his arms in Ahmadnagar, where Málik Ambár, whose tactics were those subsequently developed by the Maráthás, avoided pitched battles, but intercepted supplies, harassed marches, and made feints and attacks in turn, and so frequently as to keep the Mughal army in continual suspense. This failure was to some extent counterbalanced by the submission of the Rána of Udaipur to Prince Khurram, the Emperor's favourite son, subsequently the Emperor Shah Jahán, who had married the niece of Núr Jahán, and, from his military fame and domestic influence, was already looked on as Jahángír's successor.

The year 1616 is memorable in the Mughal annals as that in which Sir Thomas Roe arrived at the court of Jahángír as the ambassador of James I.; in England, for the death of Shakespeare; in Spain, for that of Cervantes; and in France, as the year in which the Cardinal Duc de Richelieu first received the seals of office. Roe's narrative of the court, empire, and character of Jahángír have been quoted by all subsequent writers upon this epoch, and gives a most lively and entertaining account of what he saw and experienced. The envoy travelled safely through the then disturbed tracts of the Dekhan, and noticed the alternate prosperity and decay of the different cities through which he passed—decayed cities being, it may be remarked, no great proof of want of prosperity in a country where the masses always live in lightly built and easily removed huts, and where deserted palaces are rather proofs of the fickle and unstable character of the princes, each of whom loves, if possible, to found a capital and call it by his own name. Roe admired the ruins of Mandu and Chitor, the Rana of which had defied Akbar and refused to give him his daughter in marriage. Here he met a wandering Englishman, who had walked from London to Jerusalem, and thence through Turkey and Persia to Kandahar, Lahore, and Delhi, to ride upon an elephant, which he had wagered he would do when drinking in a London tavern. He did ride upon an elephant, but died of drink at Surat before he could return to England to tell the tale. Thus were the traveller from London to Calcutta upon a bicycle, and the banjo troubadour, and the soi-disant horse-dealer of Persia anticipated. Roe made no prostration before Jahángír, but bowed, and presented a virginal, some embroidery, and of course some knives, as makers of which the English were known throughout the East; and Jahángír, when King James's envoy had left the presence, said he thought that that most high and puissant prince, had he been as great as he was represented, would at least have sent gold and precious stones. In fact, king and prince, Jahángír and Sháh Jahán were grasping and inquisitive as well as profuse and magnificent. Roe complains that a visit to the latter prince cost him a small fortune in presents to his retainers. The same thing happens to this day in Persia, where princes pay their servants more by visitors' vails than by salaries. A feature of Eastern life, which happily is not characteristic of to-day, was the execution of a hundred thieves while the court was in camp, and the arrival of camels from Kandahar bringing the heads of three hundred rebels. After a fruitless stay of three years, Roe returned to England with nothing more than a complimentary letter to King James. He had been sent in the hope of obtaining more favourable terms for English trade at Surat and on the western coast, where knives and broadcloth were exchanged for silk, spices, pepper, cotton, and precious stones. That arts and manufactures were well advanced at this time is proved by the fact that a coach Sir Thomas Roe brought for Jahángír was speedily copied and improved in Delhi, and that the pictures he brought were so reproduced that he with difficulty distinguished the copies from the originals.

In 1616 Jahángír marched to Mandu, just a little south of the Vindhya mountains, and sent Sháh Jahán still farther south to subdue the kingdoms of the Dekhan. The Prince succeeded in breaking up the confederation of the southern Sultans, and Málik Ambár at length submitted to the Mughal supremacy. But only four years later, when Jahángír was enjoying a cool summer in Kashmir, Málik Ambár again defied him, and Sháh Jahán again marched southwards, and by success in the fields of arms and diplomacy brought about a return to the previous settlement. At this time Jahangir fell ill; the usual intrigues commenced, and the sudden and opportune death of the eldest son, Khusru, was rightly or wrongly attributed to his brother, Sháh Jahán, whose fortunes were adversely affected by the determination of Núr Mahál to marry her daughter by her first husband, to his youngest brother, Shahríyár. Núr Mahál dreaded the abilities of Sháh Jahán, who had married the daughter of her brother, but was altogether unwilling to subordinate himself to the Empress's imperial will. She accordingly induced Jahángír to send him on an expedition to recover Kandahar, which the Persians had taken in 1621, and called in the governor of Kábul, Mahábat Khan, to assist her in the coming strife; for Sháh Jahán, as she expected, rebelled and seized upon the government of Bengal, from which province, however, he was expelled, and whence he retreated to the Dekhan and joined Málik Ambár, the ablest and most implacable foe of the Mughals. Prince Parviz, his brother, and Mahábat Khan opposed him, and he was soon compelled to sue for pardon, and send his sons Dárá Sheko and Aurangzeb as hostages to the imperial court; but by singular good fortune the Empress now declared against her favourite, Mahábat Khan, who had become too great to be a friend. The disgraced general was summoned to attend the Emperor, who on his way to Kábul was encamped upon the Hydaspes, which his army had already crossed. The bold design of seizing the Emperor at once occurred to the fertile mind of Mahábat, who had 5000 Rajputs under his command. He executed this perilous enterprise speedily and successfully, and was possessed of the person of Jahangir before that inebriated prince knew what was taking place. The Empress escaped unmolested across the river to the army, and during the night a desperate but unavailing effort was made to deliver the royal captive by a few horsemen who swam the storied Hydaspes. Next day Núr Jahán herself, seated upon an elephant with her grandchild in her arms, conducted the imperial army across the stream and gave battle to Mahábat and his Rajputs.

The latter, however, from the banks easily repulsed their fatigued adversaries, who buffeting their way through the river, endeavoured in vain to effect a landing. The driver of the Empress's elephant was killed and the infant in her arms wounded. When the elephant recrossed the river, Núr Jahán was found covered with blood and tending the wound of her grandchild. She then abandoned force, fell back upon woman's stronger weapon, and joined her husband to plot and scheme for his deliverance, while he and she affected submission to Mahábat's supremacy. The Khán was entirely deceived by these machinations, and Jahángír in no long time and without bloodshed was restored to authority, while Mahábat Khán joined with Shah Jahán in his rebellion, which was prosecuted the more vigorously on the death of Prince Parviz. While such was the condition of the empire, Jahángír was taken ill while marching into Kashmir, and died in 1627, in the sixtieth year of his age.

His personal character has already been described. He spent the greater part of his reign in reducing rebellions and in unrestrained self-indulgence. His total revenues have been estimated at fifty millions, and his territories were, but for the loss of Kandahár, conterminous with those of Akbar; for, in fact, he added nothing to the imperial dominions, notwithstanding his long wars in the Dekhan.

III. SHAH JAHAN (1627–1658).

Sháh Jahán reigned from 1627 to 1658, the contemporary of Charles I. and Cromwell in England, of Louis XIII. and XIV. of France, and his accession was followed by the removal of Prince Shahriyár and of the sons of Prince Dánial. Dawar Sheko or Balaki, the son of the unfortunate Khusru, fled to Persia, and neither he nor the previously all-powerful empress, Núr Jahán, again play any part in Indian history.

No sooner was Sháh Jahán firmly seated upon the throne than he indulged his love of magnificence by building palaces and holding durbars of unparalleled splendour, in the midst of which he was called to the Dekhan, where the authority of the Mughals extended only to Eastern Khándesh, the kings of Ahmadnagar and of Bijapur being independent in their own territories. The king of Golkonda, an Afghan chief, Khán Jahán Lodi, who had commanded the troops of Jahángír in the Dekhan, made common cause with the king of Ahmadnagar, but the allies were defeated at Daulatabad and Khán Jahán was slain. The king of Ahmadnagar, whose territories were now in 1630 devastated by a terrible famine and all its attendant evils, persuaded the Adil Sháhi king of Bijapur to combine with him to check the onward progress of the Mughals, which could not but result in the destruction of all the independent kingdoms in the Dekhan. But the former king was presently assassinated by his minister, who commenced to treat with the Mughal army, but his help was half-hearted, and the king of Bijapur artfully delayed negotiations with the Emperor's general till 1632, when Sháh Jahán went back to Agra. Mahábat Khán, who was left in command, failed to subdue Bijapur, and though he defeated the minister of Ahmadnagar, that monarchy was revived by Sháhji Bhonsla, with whose advent the Maráthás first appear upon the scene, destined in no long time to assume the foremost place in Indian history.

In 1635, while the struggle between Charles I. and the Parliament was becoming acute in England, Sháh

Jahán again marched into the Dekhan, put Sháhji to flight, and besieged the king of Bijapur, who consented to pay tribute to the Mughal, remaining none the less a practically independent sovereign. Sháhji then entered into the service of Bijapur. Sháh Jahán returned to Agra in 1637, after extinguishing the kingdom of Ahmadnagar, taking Bidar, and compelling the king of Golkonda, as well as the ruler of Bijapur, to pay tribute to Delhi. Fired with these successes, the Emperor proposed to conquer Balkh, and a Rajput army was despatched into that difficult country, which was only temporarily reduced, and Prince Aurangzeb's retreat through the country of the Hazaras was so much molested as to belie the supposititious voluntary surrender of his recent conquest by the Emperor, his father. In 1648 Kandahar, which had been surrendered by the Persian governor to Sháh Jahán, was retaken by the Persians, and all efforts to recover it proved unavailing, though the Princes Dárá Sheko and Aurangzeb each in turn led large armies against its walls.

A period of peace followed, during which, in 1653, the year in which Cromwell expelled the Parliament, Sháh Jahán introduced into his possessions in the Dekhan the revenue system of Rája Todar Mal. Aurangzeb was now viceroy of the Dekhan, and an opportunity was not long wanting for the interference he sought with the affairs of the Kutab Shahi monarchy of Golkonda.

The minister, Mir Jumlá, who was on bad terms with his master, appealed to Aurangzeb, who induced Sháh Jahán to intervene in the dispute. The king of Golkonda resented this insult to his independence, and the Emperor directed Aurangzeb to enforce obedience. That crafty prince simulated a march to Bengal, and suddenly returning from Masulipatam, attacked and took Haidarabad. The king, Abdulla, fled to the neighbouring fort of Golkonda, and ultimately made his submission, agreeing to pay £1,000,000 sterling as tribute to Delhi. Aurangzeb followed up this success, which did more credit to his arms than to his honour, by an unprovoked attack on Bijapur. He took Bidar, and was about to take the capital, when news arrived from Delhi, in 1657, that the Emperor was seriously ill, and had handed over the reins of government to his eldest son, Dárá Sheko, a high-spirited and open-handed prince of forty, impetuous, arrogant, and imprudent, in every way a contrast to himself. There were two other sons, Shuja, who was a *bon vivant* and a drunkard, and Murád, a brave but dull-witted and self-indulgent prince. Aurangzeb was crafty and sagacious, possessed of personal courage and of a pleasant personality, a bigoted Mussalman, zealous in prayer, abstemious in diet, unscrupulous as to the means whereby he attained his ends. He disapproved of the latitudinarian doctrines of Akbar, which his brother Dárá professed, and abhorred the Shíyya sect, to which his brother Shuja was attached.

Princes Shuja and Murád, viceroys of Bengal and Gujarat, at once rebelled against the authority of the regent Dárá, and assumed the royal style, while Aurangzeb, in collusion with Mir Jumlá, prepared his army for the struggle, while professing attachment to Murád, whom he affected to desire to place upon the throne, prior to proceeding to Mecca, there to spend a life of devotion. Shuja was defeated by Sulaiman, son of Dárá; one imperial army was dispersed at Ujain by Aurangzeb and Murád, and in 1658 Dárá's cause was irretrievably lost by his defeat near Agra. Murád fought, as he always did, with great gallantry against a force of about 120,000, and Aurangzeb resisted with no less courage the impetuous assaults of Dárá. In the end, the much smaller but more disciplined force won the day, and Aurangzeb first returned thanks to God, then saluted his brother as Padshah, and marched to Agra, to make a vain effort to bring his father over to his càuse. Finding the Emperor irrevocably committed to the cause of his eldest son, he placed him in confinement, in which he remained till his death in 1666, at the age of seventy-four. It was now Murád's turn to learn the real character of his humble helper to the throne. That unfortunate prince was interned in the fortress of Gwalior, and Aurangzeb was proclaimed Emperor in August 1658, a few days before the death of Cromwell, and an era of national prosperity closed alike in England and in India, the Mughal empire of which country attained its greatest strength and magnificence in the reign of the deposed prince. During his reign India enjoyed a comparative respite from war, and its internal government was superior to that attained under any previous king. Tavernier, the jeweller-traveller, says that Sháh Jahán was the father of his country rather than its king; but Elphinstone, after an exhaustive study of all authorities, has arrived at the conclusion that the condition of the people must have been worse than in an indifferently governed state in modern Europe, and he compares the Mughal empire at this time with that of Rome under Severus, who restored peace and prosperity to its provinces, governed with wisdom and justice, and indulged an expensive taste for building, for magnificent durbars, and for distributing *largesse* among the people. European travellers all testify to the fertility of the country, the prosperous condition of the people, and the magnificence of the cities, and Agra is said to have better deserved the name of "Half the world" than Ispahan, the royal city which then bore, and still pretends to, that proud title.

The outward and visible signs of Sháh Jahán's government were worthy of its internal greatness. He rebuilt and adorned old Delhi, and constructed its great mosque and palace, which are now admired by crowds of cold-weather travellers to India, and the three foam bells of the lovely little Masjid, which rise lightly above the stern red walls of the fort at Agra. He enjoyed a land revenue of twenty-two millions, and his celebrated peacock throne was valued by the expert Tavernier at the enormous sum of 6½ millions; but those who have seen it can only infer that the throne has greatly decreased in value since Sháh Jahán's days.

It is, however, as the builder of the Taj Mahál that this prince is best known to the Western world. This glorious edifice stands upon a terrace overlooking the Jumna, and beneath its white marble cupola repose the remains of Mumtaz Mahál, the favourite queen of Sháh Jahán. On either side of the central building rise marble minarets, and the terrace is flanked on the sides remote from garden and river by two sister mosques. Inside the lofty hall, where the cenotaph is situated within a screen of lace-like delicate carving, the walls are decorated by mosaics of flowers made of jasper, lapis lazuli, calcedony, cornelian, jade, and other stones. The whole effect is one of combined grandeur and beauty, and above all, of such simplicity as becomes a tomb; and the British Government has shown its appreciation of this masterpiece of architecture bequeathed by its predecessors, by maintaining in perfect order a Persian garden of cypresses and roses, and a marble basin of clear running water, extending from the "dream in marble" to the superb red sandstone gate, which of itself had sufficed for admiration, but for the neighbourhood of the pearl of sepulchres. Bernier, who saw it not long after it was built, thus describes the Taj:—

" C'est un grand et vaste dôme de marbre blanc, qui s'éleve à peu près de la hauteur de celui de nôtre Val de Grace de Paris, et qui est entouré de quantité de tourelles de même matière qui décendent par degrés. Quatre grandes arcades soûtiennent tout la machine, dont trois sont entierement à jour ; la quatriéme est fermée de la muraille d'une salle, accompagnée d'une gallerie, où des Mullahs entretenus lisent incessamment l'alcoran avec un profond respect en l'honneur de Taje-Mehalle. Le centre des arcades est enrichi de tables de marbre blanc, ou l'on voit entailles de grands caractères arabes de marbre noir, qui sont un très-bel effet à la veuë. L'interieur ou partie concave du dôme, et tout le mur generalement depuis le haut jusques en bas, est couvert de marbre blanc ; il n'y a endroit qui ne soit travaillé avec art et qui n'ait sa beauté particulière. L'on ne voit par tout que jachen ou jad, que de ces sortes de pierres dont on enrichit les murailles de la chapelle du Grand Duc à Florence, que jappe, et que plusieurs autres espèces de pierres rares et de prix, mises en œuvre en cent façons.

" Sous ce dôme un petite chambre qui renferme la sepulture ; je ne l'ai pas veuë par le dedans, parce qu'on ne l'ouvre qu'une fois l'année avec grande ceremonie et qu'on n'y laisse entrer aucun chrêtien, de peur, disent-ils, de profaner la sainteté du lieu ; mais à ce que j'ai pû comprendre de ce que l'on m'en a dit, il n'est rien de plus riche ni de plus magnifique."

CHAPTER VII.

MUGHALS AND MARATHAS.

I. AURANGZEB (1658–1707).

AURANGZEB'S first care was to confirm his possession of the throne. Shuja was defeated, but Dárá, who had escaped to Gujarat, endeavoured to effect an alliance with Rája Jaswant Sing, a Rajput prince who ruled over the country intervening between Ajmir and Gujarat, the governor of which latter province had undertaken to support him in striking another blow for the crown. Aurangzeb was, however, equally alive to the value of the aid of Jaswant Sing, who had commanded the imperial troops, which he and Murád had defeated. Regardless of their former enmity, he made overtures to him with such success that the Rája deserted the cause of Dárá, whom he then attacked and defeated. On his flight to Gujarat he fell in with the French physician Bernier, who subsequently served Aurangzeb for twelve years as his doctor, and who now treated the princesses of Dárá's family. The hapless prince's wife shortly died of the privations of travel, and he himself was delivered into the hands of Aurangzeb by a chieftain whose protection he sought. The Emperor determined upon his death, but affected to act upon the sentence of his legal and religious advisers, who found the prince guilty of apostasy. It was indeed true that he had adopted Akbar's idea of uniting in one general deistic religion Moslems, Parsees, Hindus, and Christians, and that his tutor, Babu Lal, had founded a deistic sect named after himself. He was put to death, and the Emperor shed tears over the head which he had ordered to be struck off. Meanwhile Shuja, pressed by Aurangzeb's general, Mir Jumlá, ex-minister of Golkonda, fled to Arakan, and was heard of no more, and Sulaiman, son of Dárá, was delivered up by the Rája of Kashmir. The prince was brought before his uncle in golden chains, and prayed to be put to death at once, and not to be compelled to drink *poust*, a compound which induced idiocy. Bernier says that Aurangzeb was moved, and promised that no *poust* should be administered, but the young prince soon met his death in the fortress of Gwalior, and Murád was executed under cover of a legal sentence, ostensibly for the murder of some insignificant person whom he had put to death when viceroy of Gujarat.

Charles II. had sat upon the throne of England a year when the Padshah securely occupied his royal cushion in Delhi after the removal of all competitors save his aged imprisoned father. In 1662 he despatched Mir Jumla upon the vain conquest of Assam, and in the same year he was taken ill, and repaired to Kashmir to recruit his health, by the advice of the physician Bernier, who, however, did but prescribe a change, in which the Mughal monarch annually indulged. While thus occupied he learnt that war had broken out between Bijapur and the Maráthás.

II. THE MARAṬHAS.

Prior to the birth of Sivaji the Maráthás had attracted but little attention. They were a race of cultivators living in the hilly country between Goa and Surat.

and the western extremity of the Dekhan plateau, and the hillmen had never been conquered either by the Mughal or the Muhammadan kings of the Dekhan. They were rude, superstitious, and grasping, loving plunder and addicted to a career of adventure. Sivaji's father was the chief of Junir, a fort a little to the north-east of Bombay, but his poor possessions were taken by the Mughals, and Sivaji was bred up as a brigand. In the use of the gun and in horsemanship he was an expert, but he could neither read nor write, though distinguished for superstitious devotion, and from the mountain fastnesses of the Western Gháts he organised a system of administrative robbery, from which those were exempt who paid his blackmail taxes.

The word Maráthá first occurs in the history of Ferishta, when that author relates the transactions of 1485, and when the Sultans of the Dekhàn had commenced to enlist these hardy warriors in their armies. When Málik Ambár was minister of Ahmadnagar, one Maloji Bhonsla was among the followers of one of his Maráthá lieutenants named Jadu Rao, and the son and daughter of servant and master marrying, the fruit of their union was Sivaji. Sháhji, the son of Maloji was, however, a considerable personage in the service of Ahmadnagar, on the fall of which monarchy he entered the service of the king of Bijapur, and was granted a jaghir in Mysore, in which was included the town of Bangalore, now assigned to the British Government by the Maharaja of Mysore, and occupied by the largest force of British and Indian troops in the Peninsula. As affairs in the southern portion of the Bijapur kingdom occupied Sháhji, he left Sivaji at Poona, where, before he attained the age of sixteen, he had made himself acquainted with the surrounding country and had gathered about him a band of devoted adherents, and by 1647 he had become independent in his father's jaghir, and had acquired possession, by fair means or foul, of several fortresses belonging to the king of Bijapur, who was too much occupied in constructing those magnificent buildings whose very ruins are stupendous, to pay much attention to the proceedings of an obscure freebooter in the mountains.

In 1648 Sivaji openly defied the court of Bijapur by capturing a convoy of royal treasure and by seizing the Northern Konkan, and he now gave a national and religious savour to his acts and deeds by assuming the character of the foe of the Muhammadan race and religion. The king of Bijapur, now thoroughly alarmed, for a while checkmated Sivaji by throwing his father into prison and threatening to put him to death unless his son's aggressions ceased, but Sivaji then offered his sword and services to Sháh Jahán, and so prevailed upon the Adil Shahi king to release Sháhji, after which he resumed his policy of persistent encroachment till 1655, when Aurangzeb arrived as viceroy of the Mughal Dekhan, and imposed a period of unwelcome rest upon his unquiet spirit. But as soon as the illness of Sháh Jahán recalled to Delhi a son, solicitous for his own interests and not for his father's health, Sivaji again commenced to annex territory belonging to the king of Bijapur, who sent Afsal Khán against him with a large force. This proud noble despised an enemy, who feigned a fear he little felt, and was inveigled into a personal interview with Sivaji, who with his own hand struck him down. He had advanced apparently unarmed, but with a dagger beneath his shirt, and steel claws concealed within the hand professing friendship, or at least submission. Afsal Khán's equally unsuspecting army was surrounded and cut to pieces. These events happened in 1659, and in 1660 and 1661 the court of Bijapur was fully occupied in the vain effort to retrieve such a disaster. In the latter year the king himself took the field, but was soon compelled to divert his attention to the suppression of rebellions in other parts of his dominions.

In 1662 a peace was arranged, in accordance with which Sivaji retained the country between the Western Gháts and the sea from Goa to Bassein, and portions of the tableland beyond the Gháts, and the historian of the Maráthás, Grant Duff, says that he now maintained an army of 7000 horse and 50,000 foot. The larger proportion of foot to horse is noteworthy, as cavalry had formerly predominated in Indian armies. With this force Sivaji now commenced to ravage the Mughal Dekhan up to the walls of Aurangabad, where Aurangzeb, its eponymous hero, had been succeeded by his uncle, Shaista Khan. The viceroy marched against the Maráthá, who retreated before him, and occupied Poona without a blow. Sivaji, however, entered the city in disguise, surprised Shaista, who escaped with a wound by letting himself down from a window, and returned openly to his fort of Singhar. The Khan suspected treachery on the part of Jaswant Sing, and their dissensions ended in the dismissal of the former to the government of Bengal, and the despatch of Prince Muázzim, Aurangzeb's son, to the command in the Dekhan, while Sivaji attacked and plundered Surat in 1664, the English and Dutch factories alone escaping his depredations. In the same year died his father, Sháhji, who, though nominally only a servant of Bijapur, had extended his conquests in the Peninsula as far south as Tanjore. In the year following Sivaji took several vessels carrying pilgrims to Mecca. He had now assumed the title of Rája, and his continued and aggravated offences against Mughal supremacy calling for decisive action, Aurangzeb replaced Jaswant Sing and Muázzim by Rája Jai Sing and Dilir Khán, who had orders to vigorously prosecute the war against Sivaji, and after his submission to conquer Bijapur. Vain hope and false policy, for he should have invoked the aid of the Muhammadan kings of the Dekhan, and have united all the Muhammadans against the Hindus of Southern India ; instead of which, he made the reduction of the independent Muhammadan kingdoms his chief aim, and in reducing them so wasted his resources and weakened his empire, that it was unable after his death to make way against the very foe he had despised.

III. AURANGZEB—(*continued*).

Sivaji, who was ever prepared to bend before a storm, made his submission to the Mughal generals in 1665, was received with great distinction by Jai Sing, and joined the imperial army in its operations against Bijapur —his enemy, be it observed, as well as theirs—his, in fact, and not really theirs, had they had the political instinct to know it. Aurangzeb thanked Sivaji for his services so cordially, and treated him with such honour, that he consented to visit the Emperor at Delhi. Here, however, his reception was such that he could not but conclude that the intention was at the least to humiliate him. His requests for leave to return were either refused or evasively answered, but, with his usual resourceful cunning and audacity, he managed to be conveyed out of the imperial city in a hamper, and made good his escape to his capital of Raighar in the Konkan in the guise of a religious mendicant.

Notwithstanding the escape of so great a foe, the

year 1666 and its immediate successors were years of prosperity in the Mughal empire, while London was devastated by fire and the Dutch defeated the English on the seas, while France under Louis XIV.'s greatest minister, Colbert, enjoyed a brief period of financial prosperity.

While, however, Little Thibet and Chittagong were added to the Mughal's dominions, his operations against Bijapur were unsuccessful, and the country surrounding the capital was devastated by the home armies, so that it could not support an invading force. The frequent resort to these tactics in some measure perhaps accounts for the barren and unproductive nature of the country, and its peculiar liability to suffer from famines, in the present day. This reverse made the Padshah willing to incline a favourable ear to Sivaji's overtures for an accommodation, and he was allowed to resume the position and title of Rája, of which all the power of the Mughals had failed to deprive him, and he soon compelled the states of Bijapur and Golkonda to pay tribute. Nor were his talents displayed only in war; he exhibited great capacity in civil and military administration, and maintained peace and security throughout his dominions, till Aurangzeb, despairing of his capture by stratagem, openly attacked him, whereupon he ravaged Khándesh, and levied *chout*, or a contribution of a quarter of the revenue, as a condition of security against attacks by the Maráthás, and in 1672 defeated a Mughal army in a pitched battle, after which military operations in the Dekhan were temporarily suspended, owing to the fact that war broke out between the Padshah and the Afghans, with whom an unsatisfactory settlement was effected after a struggle which lasted two years, during which the Emperor's troops were by no means uniformly successful. In 1676 an extraordinary insurrection broke out of Hindus, called Satnarámis, who pretended that the weapons of mere mortals were powerless against them. Aurangzeb, however, defeated them with mortal troops, fortified by texts from the Koran written with his own hand and borne upon their banners. It is stated by Elphinstone, on what authority is not known, but the fact seems that the measure was the natural outcome of the Emperor's fanatical disposition, that this rebellion led Aurangzeb in 1677 to revive the poll-tax levied in former times on others than Muhammadans. Early in his reign he had revived the use of the inconvenient Muhammadan lunar year; had suppressed gaming-houses and liquor-shops by dragonnades, and had forbidden the performances of dancing-girls and musicians. One day as he was going to his prayers, he met a crowd of men and women surrounding a bier and filling the air with wails, and asking what was the matter, was told by the mourners that they were going to bury their mother Music, who had been slain by the Padshah. He forbade the compilation of historical records—a bigoted measure which has prevented posterity from profiting to the full by his errors—and he forbade the entertainment of the Hindus in the service of the Government.

But the aggregate of these impolitic and unpopular measures was fraught with less fatal consequences to the Mugal empire than the revival of the *jaziah*, a tax imposed during the days of the early conquests of Islam on all infidels, who had either to submit to its levy or be slain. Only eight years later, the greatest monarch of Europe, as Aurangzeb then was of Asia, signed the Revocation of the Edict of Nantes, and the two events are of almost equal historical importance, and were equally fatal to the Grand Monarque and the Great Mughal. Aurangzeb, however, yielded to a nobler mentor than the bigoted wife of Louis XIV., and his error, notwithstanding the crimes which he committed to consolidate himself upon his throne, may fairly be ascribed to the promptings of a sensitive if perverted conscience.

The consequences were immediate, and precipitated the disintegrating forces at work in the empire. The Rajputs, Hindus of the Hindus, whose Rájas had, nevertheless, been among the first generals of the Mughal armies, were at once alienated, and the Maráthá freebooters became by the irony of events the champions of the Hindu religion and of the national party. The smouldering disaffection of the Rajputs was fanned into a flame by Aurangzeb's harsh treatment of the family of Rája Jaswant Sing. Several Rajput princes combined to resist the levy of the *jaziah*, and the severity with which the Emperor ravaged their territories, burnt their villages, and carried off their women and children, completed the alienation of brave allies that no government, least of all that of aliens, could afford to lose. In Jaipur the tax was collected; in Jodhpur it was redeemed by the nominal cession of a small territory; but Udaipur refused even a nominal compliance, and in the recesses of the Aravali Mountains bent before the storm it could not face, and alone engaged the forces of the empire. And now Aurangzeb had been upwards of twenty years upon the throne, when, in 1679, his sons began to follow the precedent he set them and to covet their father's crown. Prince Akbar, the second son, deserted to the Rajputs and marched against the Emperor, who, however, succeeded in bringing back to its allegiance Akbar's army, and scored a bloodless victory, while his rebellious son fled for shelter to the Maráthás. In 1681 Aurangzeb patched up an unsatisfactory peace with the Rajput princes, but all Rajputana continued to be in a state of overt or covert hostility from that time forward.

But Aurangzeb was to watch the progress of the

Maráthás and decline of the Mughal empire for twenty-eight more weary years. While he had been engaged with the Afghans and the Rajputs, Sivaji had possessed himself of the whole of the Southern Konkan, had invaded the Mughal provinces of Khándesh, Berar, and Gujarat, and, after entering into an alliance with the king of Golkonda, had started in 1677 upon a tour of conquest in the south, under the pretext of recovering the territory his father had held, nominally as a vassal of Bijapur. He took Jinji, Vellore, Arni, and Bellary, recovered all his father had ever held, and added to the family new conquests, and arranged with his brother Venkaji an amicable division of the Maráthá territories in the Peninsula.

Faithful to his mistaken policy of crushing the Muhammadan Sultans of the Dekhan, Aurangzeb had renewed in 1679 his attacks upon Bijapur, which in despair had besought the aid of its natural enemy, Sivaji, who gave it in consideration of the complete cession to him of the Bijapur territory between the Tungabadra and Krishna rivers, and of the family possessions in the south of the Peninsula, over which his brother Venkaji till then had nominally ruled. Hardly had these terms been arranged when Sivaji died in 1680, and was succeeded by his son Sambaji, who had already manifested a disposition to debauchery, and had distressed the later years of his great father by his disobedient and disloyal conduct. He confirmed the promise of his youth and signalised his ascent to the throne by the removal of his father's widow and by other cruelties, unpardonable even by the code of the age, which condoned the disappearance of all competitors for the crown. In 1682 he made an unsuccessful attempt to reduce the Abyssinians of Jinjera, a warlike maritime people who had settled on the coast opposite his capital, Raighar, and was thus engaged in the following year, when Aurangzeb left Delhi never to return, but to spend a quarter of a century in camp in the vain effort to complete the conquest of Southern India. It is easy to be wise after the event, and to express surprise that the experience of twenty-five years had not taught the Padshah that his chief foe was the wily Maráthá. He had seen the rise of the Hindu robber chief with scorn, and rather longed to destroy the proud Muhammadan monarchies that his great predecessors had failed to subdue, the importance and extent of which are to this day little realised, though they maintained their independence throughout the palmy days of the Mughal empire, and only by a little span anticipated its fall by their own. The mists of birth, prejudice, pride, and training prevented Aurangzeb from seeing in the Maráthás the cloud no bigger than a man's hand, though before this it was indeed a cloud of cognisable dimensions.

The campaign opened inauspiciously for the imperial arms by the suicide of an army under Prince Muázzim, which marched through the Konkan to Goa unopposed, but bereft of supplies, which were cut off by the Maráthás, and destroyed by hunger and fever. A year later Sambaji revenged upon the Mughals this invasion of his territory by sacking Barhampur, one of the greatest cities in the Mughal Dekhan, and again by the plunder of Broach, a success which induced an alliance with the king of Golkonda, whose territories thereupon the Padshah invaded. The king, Abul Hasan, confided the conduct of affairs to a Brahman minister, Madana Punt, who, on the approach of Prince Muázzim's army, was murdered in an émeute. The king fled to the fort of Golkonda, now the head-quarters of a brigade of the troops of His Highness the Nizam;

Haidarabad was burnt and plundered, and the king purchased peace at the price of a king's ransom.

This victory enabled the Padshah to bring all his forces to bear upon Bijapur, which underwent all the horrors of a siege. In 1686 the city was taken and sacked, and since that date it has presented the forlorn appearance of a silent assemblage of great mosques and palaces, of gems of architecture, of wondrous domes, bereft of inhabitants, standing in a vast and dreary plain, like the unreal creation of a mirage.

In the following year, regardless of treaty obligations, the Emperor, now relieved of all apprehension on the score of Bijapur, suddenly attacked Golkonda, which was bravely defended during a siege of no less than seven months, and then only taken by treachery within its walls. That treachery, however, which he welcomed among his adversaries, Aurangzeb dreaded within his house. Mindful of the rebellion of Prince Akbar, he distrusted Prince Muázzim, who, according to Bernier, gave him little ground for distrust. Successful in his wars against the Muhammadan Sultans, he destroyed the fabric which preserved order in the Dekhan, and left it the prey of the Maráthás. For a while, however, fortune smiled on the Mughal, and he possessed himself of all the territories of Bijapur and Golkonda. Thus in 1688, the year of the flight of James II. from England, the Mughal empire reached its farthest limits, and in extent of territory the Padshah of Hindustan was superior to any one of his predecessors. In the following year, learning that Sambaji was engaged in a debauch in a solitary pleasure-house, Aurangzeb directed his governor of Kolapur to make an effort to seize him, an enterprise in which that officer was completely successful. The unhappy Sambaji scornfully refused to embrace Islam, and his refusal afforded a pretext upon which to put him to death, and he was executed with great barbarity, his eyes being destroyed and his tongue cut out before he was beheaded. This act merely accentuated the religious hatred of the peoples of the Dekhan against the imperial cause, and Sambaji's son Sahu was proclaimed his successor under the regency of his uncle Rája Ram, who endeavoured to withstand the Mughals, but lost Raighar, the Maráthá capital, and retreated as far south as Jinji. The Maráthá chieftains, following their usual policy, affected to bend before the storm and pretended submission to the imperial forces, so that it appeared as if the Maráthá power had been broken in the Dekhan. But Rája Ram, whom the Mughal general Zalfikar Khán was unable to expel from Jinji, sent his two lieutenants, Santaji Gorpara and Daraji Jadu, to renew the war by organising desultory operations under individual leaders, who attracted to their standards the discharged forces of the subdued Muhammadan kingdoms of the Dekhan, and all those in search of pay and plunder, of whom the number was, in the disorganised condition succeeding to Aurangzeb's southern conquests, unusually large. Every soldier of the Maráthá had a right to levy *chout* in all non-Maráthá territories and to plunder wherever its payment was refused. A powerful army was thus called into being of active soldiers, inured to fatigue, unaccustomed to luxury, well mounted upon Dekhani ponies, and armed with sword, gun, and spear. They never attempted to face a charge, but made for ground on which the heavy Mughal cavalry could not operate, and when the enemy retired, fatigued and disheartened, they hung around and harassed their rear and plundered their convoys and commissariat. The Mughals, on the other hand, had degenerated during the comparatively peaceful reigns which preceded that of Aurangzeb, and had acquired to a great extent the somewhat ease-loving and slothful habits of their Hindu neighbours. The nobles had become debauched and effeminate and discipline had departed from among them, and the soldiers imitated the luxury of their superiors, so that the camp-followers became as a swarm of locusts which ate up the country-side, and increased a thousandfold the difficulties of transport. With such troops, and the jealousies reacting from Aurangzeb's system of divided command, the siege of Jinji lasted for no less a period than three years, when Santaji Gorpara sowed dissension between Prince Kambaksh and Zalfikar Khán, which still further postponed a successful issue. The prince was recalled by Aurangzeb, whose headquarters were now upon the Bhima river, to the east of Satára, and Jinji was left in charge of Zulfikar, who was suspected of prolonging operations in the south in expectation of the death of the aged Emperor, on the occurrence of which event he hoped to be in the position of power and influence attached to a great command. Beyond 1698, however, he could not with any regard for his reputation delay, and in that year the fortress fell. In 1700 the Padshah in person took the field, captured Satára after a siege of several months, and for four or five years persevered, in spite of his great age, in the endeavour to expel from the Dekhan his almost unresisting but ever-unconquered foe. During the acute discomforts and dangers of continuous marches in a wild country, he carried on the administration of affairs, military and civil, giving orders with his own hand concerning all the multifarious business involved in the administration of so vast an empire. Such attention to detail is hardly compatible with really efficient administration, but Aurangzeb distrusted his governors and generals, and dreaded rebellion on the part of his sons. Nor did affairs prosper, notwithstanding his industry. Revolts occurred among the Rajputs, the Jats, the Sikhs, and the Maráthás recovered one by one the forts of which they had been deprived. The state of the imperial finances became serious, and many of Aurangzeb's letters dwell upon the difficulty he experienced in getting money wherewith to pay his troops, who, in default of payment, began to desert and display a mutinous spirit. As the grand army declined in numbers, in spirit, and in efficiency, the Maráthás increased in daring, and commenced to hem it in and press it hard. Broken at last in spirit, and bowed down with age and misfortune, Aurangzeb opened negotiations for peace and such an arrangement as might save his honour, but the Maráthás demanded so much more than he could or would concede, that all hope of an amicable settlement had to be abandoned.

In 1706 the Padshah retreated to Ahmadnagar, and sickened of age and despair. His suspicions of his sons were rather increased by the approach of death, and one of them proposing a visit to Ahmadnagar for a change of air, he remarked that "no air was so unwholesome as the fumes of ambition." During his last hours he wrote letters to his sons that may reconcile the undistinguished to their lot in life. After so long a reign, extending from the time of Oliver Cromwell to that of Queen Anne, his last words were, "Wherever I look, I see nothing but God. I have committed many crimes, and know not how I shall be punished. The death-agony presses upon me; I am going. Come what may, I have launched my vessel upon the waves. Farewell, farewell, farewell."

He died on the 21st February 1707, in the eighty-ninth year of his life and the fiftieth of his reign, and in his will left instructions that only four and a half rupees, which he had earned by the work of his own hands, should be expended upon his funeral expenses. In his private habits he was simple, in his public aspects magnificent, not slothful in business, constant in prayer and supplication, a bigot, and, where political needs required, a murderer of his kindred. Elphinstone says he would have been a great king had he not had a heart cold and calculating, a stranger to all generous and ennobling impulses. On the other hand, a native historian says "that in devotion, austerity, and justice, in courage, patience, and sound judgment, he was without peer; but as from reverence to the injunctions of the Divine law he did not inflict punishment, and as without punishment no country can be kept in order, every plan and design he formed came to little good."

It is indeed the fact that the Hindus were subjected to little if any violence, though annoyed and estranged by the measures described in the preceding pages. From his letters which have been preserved, his policy of mistrust is laid bare, and his cold heart is exposed to the judgment of later days. A European traveller, Gomelli, who saw him in 1695 in old, but not in extreme old age, says he was short and stooped, had a long nose, a white skin, a round beard, and manifested an evident pleasure in the disposal of public business.

The land revenue of Aurangzeb is reported to have reached 30 millions sterling, and in the imperial accounts it was entered at 34½ millions. This was the demand upon the whole of Hindustan and all Northern India except Assam, and for Southern India, including the most southern districts. From the whole of his dominions, including Kashmir and Kabul, no less than 38½ millions were demanded. The total revenue was calculated in 1697 at 77½ millions.

Aurangzeb died while the English were engaged

against Louis XIV. in the war of the Spanish succession, in the year succeeding that in which the battle of Ramillies was fought, in the year of the Union of England with Scotland. He had himself come in contact with the English, who had taken a vessel bound from Surat to Mecca, and had seized some of their factors at his ports. The historian Kháfi Khan was sent as an envoy from the Viceroy of Gujarat to Bombay, where the English merchants told him that the ship had been taken by pirates, and that they were not responsible for the act. In fact, the seizure was probably made by some of the "interlopers," who were as much hated of the English as of the Mughal.

CHAPTER VIII.

THE MUGHALS—(*Continued*).

I. SHAH ALAM I. TO THE INVASION OF NADIR SHAH (1707–1738).

AURANGZEB had declared by his will that of his sons, Muázzim, or Sháh Alam, as Padshah, should have the northern and eastern provinces; Azim, all to the south and south-west of Agra, except Golkonda and Bijapur, which were to fall to Kambaksh; but the two elder brethren at once commenced the usual struggle for the throne. The elder, who was victorious, assumed the title of Bahádur Shah, and both his brothers were slain in fighting against him. To overthrow Kambaksh, Bahádur Shah had marched to the Dekhan, where the Maráthás were divided into parties, one upholding the cause of Sahu, the son of Sambaji, and another that of the son of Raja Ram. The Emperor left Dáud Khán in charge of the Dekhan, on behalf of Zalfikar, whom he appointed viceroy, and Dáud Khán agreed with Sahu, whose side he favoured, for the payment of *chout*, a fact which illustrates the real relative position at this time of viceroy of the Dekhan and chief of the Maráthás. The arrangement, however, gave the Emperor time to turn his attention to the Rajput princes, and, in return for a guarantee of peace, he granted to them practical independence, and marched against the

Sikhs in 1709. The Sikhs were a religious sect the founder of whose religion was Nanak Shah, who was born at Lahore in 1469. He recognised no distinction of caste, preached universal toleration and the unity of the godhead, and the necessity for a blameless life. He held that forms were immaterial and that all true worship was acceptable to God. Ten successors, ending with Guru Govind Sing, brought the line down to the date of their persecution by the successors of Aurangzeb. Immediately after the death of the great Akbar, however, the Muhammadan oppressions had commenced, and in 1675 the Guru Govind formed his followers into a religious and military commonwealth, each member of which was to be a soldier, always to wear, as the Sikhs do to this day, cold steel in some form or other about his person, and never on any pretext to shave. The Sikhs revere the Brahmans and forbid the slaughter of kine, and so far follow the law of Hinduism, but in what else they have abjured and adopted, they so differ from the Hindus as to have acquired a distinct national character. The intermittent persecution they underwent gave a more strongly fanatic cast to their character, and at last this spirit broke forth under a chief called Bandu. They rebelled in the Punjab, destroyed mosques, slew priests, sacked towns and massacred their inhabitants, so that it became necessary for Bahádur Shah to proceed against them in person. He drove them into the hill country and imposed a temporary check upon their aggressions, when in 1712 his short reign of five years was ended by his death. He had been the contemporary of Queen Anne, who survived him, however, by two years.

After the usual struggle, his eldest son, Jahandar Shah, succeeded to the throne by the help of Zalfikar Khan, whom he appointed his Minister. He was a profligate prince, and alienated the nobility by promoting to the highest rank and position the relatives of his mistress, a dancing-girl. His nephew, Faroksir, supported by the brothers Sayyid Husain Ali and Sayyid Abdulah, governors of Behar and Allahabad respectively, rebelled, defeated the Emperor, and put him and Zalfikar Khan to death, and ascended the throne in 1713, a year of no great note in India, but famous in Europe as that of the Peace of Utrecht.

The Sayyids now succeeded to the position of king-maker lately held by Zalfikar Khan, and their nominal sovereign soon began to weary of their ascendency, and sent Husain Ali to the Dekhan as viceroy, secretly instructing the deceased Zalfikar's lieutenant, Dáud Khán, to oppose him. This Dáud did with a reckless courage, which defeated his master's object as well as his enemy's troops. He was slain on the field, and the obnoxious Sayyid continued to hold the high office conferred upon him by his perfidious master. The Sikhs now again attacked the imperial troops and stations. They were defeated, and their chief Bandu and many others taken prisoners. Seven hundred and forty were beheaded in Delhi, not one of whom would save his life by abjuring his religion. Bandu himself was torn to pieces with hot pincers, after his child's heart had been thrown in his face, but to the last breath he gloried in his religion, and thanked God that he was destined to be its martyr-witness. The Sikhs were hunted down like wild beasts, and these severities led to their temporary disappearance from the scene.

The Mughals at this period revenged upon the Sikhs their impotence to deal with the Maráthás. Chin Kilich Khán, better known as Asof Jáh and Nizam-ul-Mulk, had been able by cunning rather than by arms to prevent the further progress of the Maráthás, but when he was succeeded by Husain Ali, their ravages were unchecked, and after one ineffectual attempt at resistance, Husain by treaty with Sahu acknowledged his claim to all the territories ever occupied by Sivaji, to all the later conquests of the Maráthás, and agreed to pay *chauth* for the whole of the Dekhan. True, Rája Sahu was to pay a tribute of ten lakhs of rupees, but this was an absolutely ludicrous return, and only stipulated for in order in some measure to preserve appearances in the negotiation of these humiliating terms, which the Emperor refused to confirm.

This refusal and his jealousy of the Sayyid brothers led to continual plots and counter-plots, the Emperor forming combinations for the purpose of ridding himself of his hated protectors and patrons, but lacking the courage to carry them into effect. The Sayyids therefore resolved upon his death, and as his adherents all forsook so craven a prince, he was quietly strangled in his zenana in 1719. They then elevated to the throne two young princes named Rafi-ud-Dirjat and Rafi-ud-Daulat, who died within a few months, and subsequently another named Raushin Akhtar, who was crowned under the title of Muhammad Shah. The government of the Sayyids, however, fell into disrepute, and insurrections against themselves and their puppet king broke out on all sides, and Chin Kilich Khan, or Asof Jáh, determined to make himself independent in his old viceroyalty of the Dekhan. In 1720 he defeated two armies sent against him by the brothers, and openly defied their power and that of the Emperor.

Asof Jah thus founded the line of the Nizams of the Dekhan, powerful princes, who made treaties with the English on equal terms, and whose court is now perhaps as splendid as that of any Muhammadan prince, excepting only the Sultan. He possessed bravery and cunning in equal measure, and alone of the great nobles of the court had the spirit to resent an insult offered to him by the favourite of the low-born mistress of Jahandar.

Meanwhile Muhammad Sháh found intolerable the tutelage he had supported with difficulty since his accession. In conjunction with Sadat Khán it was decided to assassinate the Sayyids. Husain Ali was accordingly poniarded in his palanquin by a pretended petitioner. His brother Abdullah attempted to maintain the falling fortunes of his house, but was defeated by the Emperor in a battle fought between Delhi and Agra. Muhammad was so far successful, but revolts broke out among the Rajput princes, and it was obvious that the central power was wholly unable to enforce its authority in the provinces. Asof Jáh, after securing his independence in the Dekhan, returned to Delhi as Minister, where he found all in confusion, and the Emperor, the slave of his mistress, who kept his seal and exercised his powers. Mutual recriminations and distrust soon succeeded, and in 1723 the Minister resigned and returned to his government of the Dekhan. The Emperor instigated the governor of Haidarabad to oppose him, whereupon Asof Jáh gave him battle, defeated him, and sent his head to the Emperor as that of a rebel.

He then turned his attention to his really powerful enemies, the Maráthás. He had during his first government of the Dekhan busily fomented the dissensions consequent upon the rival claims of Sahu and Samba to the throne of Sambaji. The chief authority, however, resided at this time in the Brahmin Bálají Visvanáth, originally a village accountant in the Konkan, who supported the cause of Sahu, confirmed him in his throne, and became his Peshwa or Minister. He obtained from Muhammad Sháh confirmation of the treaty legalising the levy of *chauth*, which Farokhsir had refused to ratify, and endeavoured to introduce some system into the complicated finances of the Maráthá administration. He claimed as *chauth* one quarter of the revenue as fixed by Todar Mall and Malik Ambar; but as the distracted country yielded but a fraction of that revenue, he took what he could get, an indefinite and unsettled demand being dearer to a race of free-booters than a fixed contribution, especially when without force neither could be levied, and when an ill-defined claim afforded a welcome pretext for continual interference. The different heads of revenue in one and the same district were assigned to different chiefs for collection, which prevented any one collector from becoming independent of the central government, the necessity for which measure was apparent from the recent experience of the Mughal in the Dekhan. The intricacy of the accounts which resulted from the adoption of this system led to the universal appointment of Brahmin accountants, then as now the only class in India that can deal with complicated figures, and so increased the Brahmin ascendency which Bálají had so much at heart. Bálají died in 1720, and was succeeded as Peshwa by Báji Rao, the able son of an able sire, who urged a bold and forward policy. Grant Duff, the historian of the Maráthás, records that in the divided counsels of the chiefs he advised an invasion of the northern provinces of the Mughal empire, saying, "Let us strike the withered trunk, and the branches will fall of themselves." In accordance with this counsel, at once bold and prudent, Báji Rao ravaged Malwa, levied *chauth* in Gujarat, compelled Asof Jáh to relinquish the cause of Samba, who still urged his claims to the Maráthá throne, and forced the latter to content himself with the empty title of Rája and a small territory around Kolapur.

Asof Jáh endeavoured without ceasing to foment dissensions among the Maráthás, and it was at his instigation that the hereditary commander-in-chief of the forces fell upon the Peshwa, marching from Gujarat for the purpose with a powerful army. The Peshwa, however, attacked and defeated him in 1731 before Asof Jáh had time to effect a junction with his troops. The chief of the rebellion was slain in the battle, but his son was confirmed in the rights of the Maráthás over Gujarat, with the important difference, that half the revenues were to be paid through the Peshwa to the Government. The son, however, was a minor, and the real power fell into the hands of Pilaji Gáekwar, whose descendant is the present Gáekwar of Baroda, who, so greatly have Indian princes changed in 160 years, spends many of his summers in England, and makes an excellent speech at a Guildhall banquet. At or a little before this time, the ancestors of Mahárájas Holkar of Indore and Sindia of Gwalior rose to eminence as lieutenants of Báji Rao. The former was originally a shepherd, and the latter a servant of the Peshwa.

A treaty was now effected by Báji Rao with Asof Jáh, in accordance with which the Peshwa and Nizam were alike to be allowed, each by the other, to aggrandise themselves at the expense of the Mughal. Of this liberty Báji Rao availed himself to the full, expelled the Mughal governors from Gujarat and Malwa, took Bandalkand, and demanded further cessions. The Emperor, thoroughly alarmed, now sought the aid of his rebellious Minister, Asof Jáh, Nizam-ul-Mulk, and a temporary success was achieved by Sadat Khán, governor of Oudh, which, however, was only followed by the appearance of Báji Rao, with a large army before Delhi in 1737. Asof Jáh now marched northwards to assist Sadat Khán in opposing the Maráthás, but he was attacked by the Peshwa near Bhopal, and forced to cede all the Mughal territories lying between the Narbada and the Chambal rivers.

II. NADIR SHAH THE PERSIAN (1738–1739).

But India was now upon the eve of another invasion such as that of Tamarlane, which for awhile silenced all merely local strife. In order to comprehend the inroad of Nadír Sháh, a brief digression into the history of the neighbouring kingdom of Persia is necessary.

The Safavi dynasty had now fallen into decay and impotence, but Sháh Hosain none the less sent a considerable army to Kandahár to punish the Ghiljis, the most important of the tribes that occupy the western portion of the tableland of Herat, the eastern portion of which formed a kind of neutral ground between the Persian and the Mughal monarchies. At first Sháh Hosain was successful, but in 1708 his troops were expelled from Kandahár, and the Ghiljis joining for the present the Abdalis, took Herat, overran Khorassan in 1716, after which the Ghiljis, under Mahmúd, their chief, invaded Persia proper, and, after a long siege, in 1722 took the capital, Ispahan, then one of the greatest cities in the East, and even in its decay a place of some importance. For two years Mahmúd was practically king of Persia, an Afghan shepherd in the seat of Darius; and his nephew, Ashref, quietly succeeded him, and successfully opposed a combination of Turks and Russians, who agreed among themselves to dismember and divide the realm of Persia. Tahmasp, the son of Sháh Hosain, had fled for protection to the Turki tribe of Kajar, to which the present Sháh Nasr-ud-din belongs. His cause was espoused by Nadír Kuli, a freebooter of the stamp of Sivaji, who drove out the Ghiljis, and Ashref their chief, defeated the Abdalis, another Afghan tribe of the Herat tableland, who had encroached upon Khorassan, deposed Tahmasp, who till now had been his nominal sovereign, and in 1736 assumed the style of Sháh-in-Sháh, and rashly promised to perform the impossible—to establish the Sunni faith in Persia, the home of the Shiyya sect of Muhammadans—a step which showed, like others in his life, that in the warrior was found no leaven of the statesman and administrator. Flushed with successes in the field, hailed as the saviour and regenerator of Persia, in 1738 he revenged upon the Ghiljis the insults they had offered to his prostrate country, and recovered Kandahár, while his son conquered Balkh and defeated the king of Bokhara upon the Oxus.

Whether or not a reason was considered necessary by Nadír for attacking the distracted empire of the Mughals, his presence upon its frontier soon afforded him a pretext for aggression and for the employment of his arms. He applied to Delhi for the expulsion of some of his Afghan enemies, who had taken refuge in Ghazní, and when no answer was returned, sent an envoy, who was taken by the Afghans on his way to the court; whereupon he took Kábul, and, unmolested by the Afghans of the frontier, whose subsidies the Mughals had neglected to pay, he passed through the mountains, crossed the Indus, and defeated Muhammad at Kurnal, about a hundred miles from Delhi, in February 1739. Sadat Khán, viceroy of Oudh, was taken prisoner, and Asof Jáh, Nizam of the Dekhan, was despatched to offer the Padshah's submission. The invading army has been differently estimated at 160,000 and 65,000, from which it may be inferred that no reliable information is available on the subject.

In March the conquering and the captive kings were in residence in Delhi, when a false report of the former's death inspired the city folk to rise against the intruders, many of whom fell victims to the popular fury. Nadír Sháh appears to have been inclined to tolerant and even lenient measures, but when one of his captains was shot by his side, he ordered a general massacre, which lasted half the day, and in which it is believed that 30,000 persons were slain, though some historians have made the number 160,000. It is certain that bloodshed and rapine raged till the Persian king ordered its cessation, by the request, as is stated, of Muhammad Shah himself, who with tears in his eyes entreated the conqueror to spare his subjects. With Nadír Sháh, as with Mahmúd of Ghazní, though here all resemblance ceased, avarice was the ruling passion. He seized the treasures of Delhi and the peacock throne, on which the Kajar Sháh now sits in Teheran, and levied pitiless contributions upon the unhappy inhabitants, upon the governors and viceroys, upon all who would or could not pay. At last, unable to extort more from the wretched country, he left Delhi with a treasure of many millions sterling, after placing Muhammad again upon his desecrated throne, and extorting from him a treaty whereby he ceded to the conqueror everything west of the Indus.

III. To the Battle of Panipat (1761).

Hardly had the Persians devastated the provinces the Maráthás had so far spared, and departed, when the latter enemies prepared to renew their depredations. Death, which in the midst of his successes he said "he wished he could meet," removed Báji Rao in 1740 from a complicated scene, in which his active and intriguing brain had taken perhaps the foremost part. He left two legitimate sons, Bálají and Ragunátha or Ragoba, the former of whom succeeded him as Peshwa. During the last years of Baji Rao's life he had been occupied with wars in the Konkan. The pirate chief Angria of Kolába had been attacked by English, Portuguese, Dutch, and Maráthás, and yet continued his career of piracy along the western coast. The Abyssinians of Jinjera resisted all efforts to reduce them; the Portuguese had lost to the Maráthás several of their west-coast ports, but had afforded to their adversaries but Pyrrhic victories.

In the midst of these wars Bálají succeeded his father; nor were domestic difficulties absent, for the Gáekwar and Ragoji Bhonsla were powerful enemies of his house, and his treasury was empty. Yet he at once revived all Báji Rao's demands against the court of Delhi, and for the cession of Malwa, aided the Mughal viceroy of Bengal, Alí Vardi Khán, to resist the invasion of his enemy, Ragoji, who was defeated and driven out of the province, but to whom he subsequently ceded the *chauth* of Bengal and Bihar, in order to detach him from combinations with the Gáekwar and his other domestic foes. Ragoji now turned his attention exclusively to Bengal, of the *chauth* of which, and of the province of Kuttak, he soon obtained possession. In the Dekhan, Asof Jáh died in 1748, and Sahu Raja in the following year. Bálají seized upon the government, and proclaiming as Rája the grandson of Tára Bai, widow of Rája Ram, in order that he might exercise the power of king in his name, he confirmed Ragoji Bhonsla in all he held, and made great concessions to Sindia and Holkar, as the price of their countenance of his proceedings. The intestine feuds of the Maráthás have no place in this work, but this led to the invasion of the Maráthá dominions by Salabat Jung, third son of Asof Jáh, who had succeeded his father, aided by a French force under Bussy. Salabat and Bussy had advanced in 1751 to the neighbourhood of Poona, when a mutiny in Salabat's army forced him to retire.

Meanwhile Nadír Sháh had been occupied in the conquest of Bokhara and Kharizm in a campaign against the Turks. He had alienated the Persians by his atrocious cruelties, and by his suppression of the Shiyya religion. A mutual feeling of distrust culminated in his assassination in 1747 by the officers of his own guard, whereupon Ahmad Khán, chief of the Abdalis or Duránis, caused himself to be crowned king at Kandahar, and asserted over the Afghan tribes such loose and ill-defined sovereignty as those hardy and independent tribesmen will endure. He succeeded, in fact, to the authority of Nadír Sháh in the countries between the Indus and the Persian frontier and in Khorassan, the dissensions of the Persians preventing any serious opposition on their part. In the year following his assumption of the regal dignity he invaded the Punjab, but was driven back by the heir-apparent, Prince Ahmad, who in 1748 succeeded Muhammad Shah, upon the death of that sovereign, after a disastrous reign of twenty-nine years.

Ahmad Shah appointed Safdar Jung, viceroy of Oudh, his minister, and their first effort was directed against the Rohillas, Afghans from the north-west, who had settled upon the borders of Oudh. The minister, unsuccessful in the campaign, resorted to the now familiar expedient of calling in the aid of the Maráthás. With the assistance of Holkar and Sindia he defeated his enemies, and authorised his allies to levy *chauth* throughout their territories.

And now Ahmad Sháh Duráni a second time invaded the Punjab, and the Emperor, mindful of the result of Nadír Sháh's invasion, speedily complied with his demand for the cession of that province. The minister, affecting to consider this proceeding derogatory to what remained of the dignity of the empire, relations between him and his feeble master soon became so strained that the latter incited Ghazi-ud-dín, the grandson of Asof Jáh, to oppose him by force, whence ensued the deplorable spectacle of civil war in the streets of Delhi, which was only ended by the intervention of the Maráthás under Holkar, who expelled Safdar Jung and drove him to his viceroyalty of Oudh. But whichever faction triumphed, the fate of the miserable Padshah was to be its slave, and his plots against his own creature, Ghazi-ud-dín, ended in his deposition by that ungrateful chief.

Ghazi-ud-dín, upon the death of Safdar Jung, whose son, Siráj-ud-daula, succeeded him in Oudh, took upon himself the office of minister, placed one of the princes of the blood upon the throne, with the style of Alamgír II. —the first Alamgír is better known as Aurangzeb—and proceeded to involve the fallen empire in fresh calamities by treacherously seizing the governor placed in charge of the Punjab after its cession to Ahmad Sháh Duráni. That powerful monarch immediately resented this insult by again, for a third time, invading the Punjab. He took Delhi almost without opposition, levied contributions far and wide, and rendered himself odious throughout India by the massacre of the unoffending pilgrims at Muttra, when the advent of the hot season of 1757 compelled him to return to his own cool country. He left a Rohilla chieftain, Najib-ud-daulat, behind him in command at Delhi, but hardly had he left when Ghazi-ud-dín called in the Maráthá Peshwa's brother, Ragoba, to assist him in recovering his authority. With this assistance he expelled Najib-ud-daulat and forced himself as minister upon the impotent Emperor, while Ragoba seized Lahore from Ahmad Shah Duráni's son Timur, took possession of the Punjab, threatened Oudh, and openly avowed the design of conquering all Hindustan. The Muhammadan princes were attempting to bring about a combination to prevent this consummation, when, in 1759, Ahmad Shah, for the fourth time, in 1759, invaded the Punjab to avenge the expulsion of his son. He crossed the Indus near Attok and marched to the neighbourhood of Kàrnál and Pánípat, the fateful battlefield of India. Ghazi-ud-dín, fearing an amicable settlement between Alamgír II. and the invader, put the former to death. Ahmad Sháh defeated the Maráthá troops in Hindustan under Sindia and Holkar in two separate engagements. The Peshwa's cousin, Sedasheo Rao Bháo, was now deputed to face the enemy, for the Maráthás, and not the Mughals, were the only foes Ahmad Shah had to fear.

Their power had now reached its highest point, and the whole of the late empire of the Mughals, and a far larger territory than ever acknowledged that authority in the south of India, either belonged to, or paid tribute to, the Maráthás, when Sedasheo Bháo marched northwards, and easily took from the Duráni garrison the imperial capital, the beautiful buildings of which suffered more at his Vandal hands than they had at those of foreign invaders. Ahmad Sháh having arranged with Siraj-uddaula that he should at least be neutral in the approaching contest between his co-religionists and his fellow-countrymen, marched towards Delhi, while the Maráthás entrenched themselves at Panipat, and protected their trenches with a park of artillery. Their forces have been estimated at a figure varying from 270,000 to 300,000, and those of the Duránis at 90,000 men, including Rohillas and Indian allies. The invaders soon learnt from their enemies the Maráthá system of cutting off supplies, and the host of Sedasheo soon began to feel the pinch of want.

Meanwhile Ahmad Sháh was unwearying and unceasing in his care of his troops and in his observation of the enemy. The Bháo endeavoured to gain Siráj-ud-daula over to his side, and employed as his emissary Kasi Rai, the historian, from whose narrative the events of this period have for the most part been compiled. The Indian allies of Ahmad Sháh, however, fearing the vengeance of the Maráthás if the Sháh returned, leaving their power unbroken, opposed all overtures for an accommodation.

In January 1761, the position in the Maráthá camp had become intolerable, and the Maráthás forced their chief to give battle. Siráj-ud-daula, who had now openly gone over to Ahmad Sháh, though he did not help him in the battle, informed the king of this decision, and he, nothing loth, on the morning of the 6th prepared for an engagement. The Maráthás at first had the advantage, but Ahmad Sháh, by a dexterous flank attack, changed the fortune of the day, and the forces of the Bháo fled on every side. The fugitives were cut down by thousands, alike by the enemy and by the peasants of the country-side, who had suffered from their enforced levy of supplies and plundering expeditions. The Bháo himself and Visvas Rao, the Peshwa's nephew, were among the slain, whose number has been estimated by the accurate Grant Duff at not less than 200,000. The Peshwa died of a broken heart, and the remains of his armies retreated south of the Narbada, relinquishing all their conquests in Hindustan. The dynasty of the Peshwa and the monarchy of the Mughals were alike extinguished by this battle. The Maráthás, under individual chieftains, recovered much of their territories, but the Mughal empire was irretrievably broken up into independent states, with which, and with the fortunes of the Europeans who rose to greatness upon the ruins of two thrones, the subsequent history of India is chiefly concerned.

CHAPTER IX.

CONCLUSION.

I. GROWTH OF THE BRITISH POWER IN HINDUSTAN.

THE battle of Pánípat was fought in the first year after the accession of George III., while England was engaged in the Seven Years' War. The painful death-throes of the Mughals were almost contemporaneous with the achievements of Lord Clive, whereby the empire of India fell to the English, and not to their rivals in every clime, the French, and whereby a company of traders was converted into a great Government.

It was not till the reign of Charles II. that the East India Company, formed in the reign of Queen Elizabeth, became rich and powerful enough to obtain a new charter and the cession of Bombay, the marriage portion of the Queen. Fort St. George had then been founded, but it was subsequently to the Revolution in 1698 that a grant on the Hugli was obtained from Aurangzeb. The French alone seriously competed with the English in India, where they possessed Chandernagore upon the Hugli, and Pondicherry upon the Coromandel coast. In 1746 the French took Madras, which was restored at the peace of Aix-la-Chapelle in 1748, but the real struggle commenced afterwards between Dupleix and Clive, the former endeavouring by intervention in the disputed successions to the thrones of fragments of the Mughal empire, Haidarabad and Arcot, to found a French empire in

India. The bold defence of Arcot by Clive, ten years before the battle of Pánípat, caused English influence to predominate upon the Madras coast; and in 1760, one year before that great engagement, the defeat of Lally by Coote at Wandiwash left the English masters in the south. In Bengal the tyranny of Siráj-ud-daula, the grandson of Alí Vardí Khán, the viceroy of Bengal referred to in the last chapter, and the occurrence of the Seven Years' War in Europe, led to the defeat of the Bengal viceroy by Clive at Plassey in 1757, and to the first extensive grant of territory to the English in Hindustan, which was largely increased in the year of the battle of Pánípat, when the English dethroned the viceroy or Nawab Mir Jafir. Their nominee, Mir Kasim, however, endeavoured to assert his independence, and joined with Siráj-ud-daula, the minister, and Sháh Alam, the nominal Emperor, which brought the latter into collision with the English, who defeated him at Buxar in 1764. In the following year Clive restored Oudh to the Nawab minister, and made over a fragment of the empire to Sháh Alam, in return for which that shadowy potentate granted to the English the fiscal administration of Bengal, Bihar, and Orissa, and this divided system obtained till the appointment of English collectors by Warren Hastings, who abolished the dual administration, and when Sháh Alam was seized by the Maráthás in 1773 sold the districts Clive had made over to that prince to the Nawab of Oudh, holding that neither territory nor tribute could be paid by the British to the Maráthás.

II. The British and the Marathas.

After the battle of Pánípat, Madhu Ráo had succeeded as fourth Peshwa, but the Maráthá power was divided between himself and the Bhonslas at Nagpur, the Sindias at Gwalior, Holkar at Indore, and the Gáekwar at Baroda. In 1772 the fifth Peshwa was assassinated, and in the previous year Sindia and Holkar affected to restore to the throne of Delhi Sháh Alam, who had been a British pensioner since his defeat seven years before at Baxar. In fact, they kept him prisoner in their hands till the second Maráthá war, and they continue to rule as feudatory princes in their respective capitals to the present day. The power of the Bhonslas was broken by the third Maráthá war, and on the death of the last of the house in 1853, their territory, now known as the Central Provinces, lapsed to the English, but the Gáekwar still reigns at Baroda. The guardian of the sixth Peshwa at Poona called in the French to resist a claim by his uncle. The English at Bombay opposing them, the first Maráthá war ensued (1779–1791), of which the results were but small.

From 1780 to 1784, and from 1790 to 1792, the British were, owing to the unskilful operations of the Madras Government, engaged in war with Haidar Ali, a Muhammadan adventurer, who had founded a powerful kingdom in Mysore, and with his son, Tippu. The Nizam of the Dekhan, the greatest Muhammadan, and the Maráthá confederacy, the greatest Hindu power in India, cooperated with the English to subdue Tippu, who purchased peace by the cession of half his dominions, which was divided among the allies. In 1799 he was crushed by Lord Wellesley, who determined that the sovereignty of India should pass neither to independent Muhammadan or Hindu houses, nor to the Maráthá confederacy, but to the English; in pursuance of which policy he also brought under British authority those fragments of Mughal and Maráthá rule represented by the Nawabship of Arcot and the Principality of Tanjore. Lord Wellesley's second Maráthá war of 1802 to 1804 is relevant to this narrative, because it resulted in the Emperor Sháh Alam being once more restored to the protection of the British by the Maráthá princes, who suffered defeat at their hands.

Not only the Maráthás, but the Pindarris also, disturbed the peace of India at this time. They were the camp-followers of the Maráthás, the floating residuum of India, disbanded mercenaries, and the debris of the Mughal empire, bands of plunderers who swept across India, assimilating the worst of all they came across in their raids. They were not dispersed without difficulty, after a regular campaign, by Lord Hastings in 1817. In the same year the last Maráthá war broke out between the powers of Poona, Nagpur, and Indore and the British, which resulted in the annexation of the Peshwa's dominions to the Bombay Presidency.

III. The British and the Afghans.

The British Government, which thus became paramount over the greater part of India, while the states of Rajputana also acknowledged its supremacy, had to fight again with the Muhammadans. It has been already stated that the conqueror of Pánípat, Ahmad Sháh Duráni, before he died in 1773, ruled from Herat to Pesháwar, and from Kashmir to Sindh—a wide and extensive kingdom. His capitals were Kábul and Kandahár, and after his death wars of succession were bloody and continuous between his descendants. It is not necessary here to follow these intestine feuds, and it will suffice to say that in 1809 a British mission was sent to Shuja Sháh Duráni to establish a defensive alliance; that Sháh Shuja was afterwards driven out of Kábul, and that Dost Muhammad, of the Barahzai family, had established himself as king in Kabul in 1826, when the Duráni claimant was an exile in India under British protection. All fear of Afghan invasions of India had disappeared in consequence of the establishment of the strong Sikh kingdom of Ranjít Sing in the Punjab, but Dost Muhammad's dearest object in life was the recovery of Pesháwar from the Sikhs. Lord Auckland was unable to make over to its enemies a town which belonged to an independent prince, and without this Dost Muhammad would give no satisfactory guarantees on other matters which the Governor-General had more at heart. Lord Auckland resolved to replace him by Sháh Shuja, who might reasonably be expected to be sufficiently subservient to his benefactors. That prince was accordingly placed upon the throne by British bayonets in 1839. But the Afghans would have none of him, and the British army continued for two years in Afghanistan till the Political Agents, Sir Alexander Burnes and Sir William Macnaughten, were assassinated, the latter by a son of Dost Muhammad. Under a promise that it would not be molested, the army set out for India in winter, 4000 men and 12,000 camp-followers, nearly all of whom were either slain or perished of cold and exposure on the way. This disaster was avenged in 1842 by the army of retribution under Generals Pollok and Sale.

The conquest of Sindh in 1843, and the first and second Sikh wars in 1845 and 1848–1849, the second Burmese war of 1852, the annexation of Oudh in 1856, the conflagration of the mutiny in 1857, the transfer of India to the crown in 1858, these great events succeeded one another in rapid succession before Lord Lawrence acknowledged

Sher Ali as Amir of Afghanistan, after a fratricidal war between the sons of Dost Muhammad. His successor, Lord Mayo, met Sher Ali at Umballa. It was the constant desire of the last-named eminent administrator to draw more closely the bonds of affection between the British and the native princes, but subsequently the Amir was found to have been engaged in intrigues with Russia. Sir Neville Chamberlain, who was sent as British envoy, was refused admission to Afghanistan, and war was declared by Lord Lytton in 1878. Sher Ali fled the country, and Yakub Khan, his son, consented by the treaty of Gundamuk to receive a British Resident. Hardly, however, had Sir Louis Cavagnari been in Kabul a few months, when he and his escort were assassinated. Yakub Khán then abdicated, and Kábul and Kandahár were occupied by the British. A temporary reverse between Kandahár and the Helmand river was more than retrieved by the march of Lord Roberts from Kábul to Kandahár, and the defeat of Ayub Khán in September 1880. Abdul Rahman Khán, the representative of the line of Dost Muhammad, was next recognised by Lord Ripon as Amir. He was subsequently received with great splendour by Lord Dufferin at Rawalpindi, at a time when a collision with Russia seemed only too likely after the Panjdih incident, which interrupted the delimitation of the Russo-Afghan frontier, and he still rules with vigour and success the turbulent tribes of Afghanistan.

IV. Present Condition of Indian Muhammadans.

The history of the Muhammadan epoch has now been briefly narrated from the first arrival of the followers of the Prophet through the rise and fall of the Mughal empire to the present day, contemporaneous history in India having been briefly, and outside India even more briefly noticed.

This is not the occasion for any description of the present condition of the 57,365,000 Muhammadans now in India, for which reference should be made to works specially bearing upon that subject. The Marquis of Salisbury recently described the Indian Muhammadans as a race distinguished by the great qualities of martial and statesmanlike capacity, possessed of a splendid history. Though they imposed upon India a foreign yoke, they gave it at least for a season peace, and they brought about a reform in Hinduism, by affording to the Hindus the spectacle of a nation whose guiding principle is a belief in the unity of God, while the tolerance of the Hindus reacted upon themselves, and softened the ferocity of the early Arab proselytism. Though they have not availed themselves of Western education as the more adaptable Brahmans have, yet has the number of Muhammadans at school increased from 28,000 to 850,000 in twenty years, while further progress may be confidently expected. If proud and haughty, the Indian Muslims are none the less temperate, brave, and charitable, generally speaking admirable in the domestic relations of life, and for the most part husbands of one wife, and innocent of the vices characteristic of a corrupt civilisation. Amongst the rich no doubt polygamy obtains, but the rights of women in India, as elsewhere in the Muhammadan world, are well defined, and without difficulty enforced. Efforts are made by the Government of India to ensure to this class of its subjects a due share of official preferment; and though it must be admitted that the objects of its solicitude have hardly responded by so vigorous an educational effort as might have been expected, it must also be allowed that the Queen-Empress has no more loyal subjects in India than these descendants of a race which governed the country with varying success, and through various fortunes, in the period preceding the British supremacy.

INDEX

THE END.